HOW TO RUN
FASTER

A publication of
Leisure Press
P.O. Box 3; West Point, N.Y. 10996

ISBN 0-88011-057-0
Library of Congress Number 82-81448

Figure Illustrations by John Jett

Cover photo by David Madison

HOW TO RUN FASTER

Step-by-step instructions
on how to increase foot speed.

George B. Dintiman, Ed.D.

LEISURE PRESS

NEW YORK

CONTENTS

PREFACE

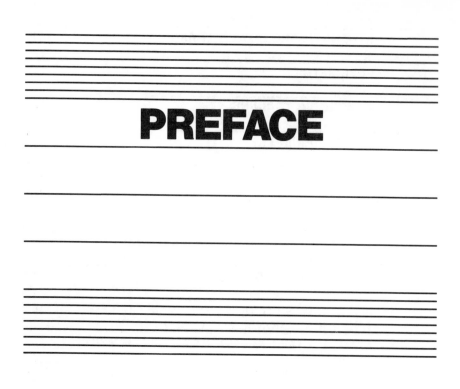

This may be the most important book you will ever read in your entire athletic career. It is the only book ever written that gives you a step-by-step program to improve your speed in short distances for football, baseball, basketball, soccer, tennis, lacrosse, rugby, field hockey, and ice hockey. Speed in short distances is your greatest asset. The faster, more powerful runner in practically any sport has the edge and becomes the better player. You can easily improve your speed by following the programs in this book that will train you to take longer steps, faster steps, more powerful steps, and to accelerate faster from a stationary position. The most modern European and American Techniques (Russian Plyometrics, Towing, Treadmill Sprinting, Downhill Sprinting, Strength/Power Training, Form Training, and Sprint Training) are discussed with step-by-step instructions that allow you to adapt training programs to your particular strengths and weaknesses.

Dr. George B. Dintiman

THE AUTHOR

George B. Dintiman, Ed.D. is Chairman of the Division of Health and Physical Education at Virginia Commonwealth University. His educational background includes a B.S. from Lock Haven State College, M.A. from New York University and Ed.D. from Columbia University.

Dr. Dintiman is a former little All-American in football, basketball, and track and a professional draft choice of the Baltimore Colts and Montreal Alouettes. He is the author of eleven books on health, fitness, and sports, three in the area of speed, and is recognized as an international authority on the improvement of sprinting speed for team sport athletes.

DEDICATION

To One of the Fastest:
My Father, George Byers Dintiman

SECTION I:
YOUR
COMPLETE
PROGRAM

1
INTRODUCTION: CAN SPEED REALLY BE IMPROVED ?

In sports at all competitive levels (age group, junior and senior high school, college or university, and professional) every athlete can benefit from additional speed in short distances. There is no single greater concern among these athletes than *how to run faster* in short distances such as the 40-yard dash. Why does this concern exist? Because without adequate speed and quickness, stardom in most sports is nearly impossible. It is THE single greatest asset you can possess in football, basketball, soccer, baseball, field hockey, rugby, lacrosse, ice hockey and tennis.

The important thing for you to recognize is that speed can be improved with proper training. Although your genetic make-up determines your maximum potential, considerable improvement is possible. In fact, some unfavorable aspects of your genetic make-up that restrict speed, such as slow-twitch muscle fiber, can even be altered. This chapter discusses these limiting factors, describes the physical characteristics that are ideal for sprinting short distances and clarifies how you can change your body for maximum improvement of speed.

World Records

A brief review of world records makes it clear that man has improved his speed in short distances through the years although the improvement is much less dramatic than in the one mile run. In 1890, the world's fastest human was John Owen who ran the 100-yd dash in 9.8. A 9.6 was recorded by Archie Hahn in 1902, lowered to 9.5 in 1926 by Charlie Paddock, lowered again to 9.3 in 1948 by Mel Patton, continuing to 9.2 in 1962 (Frank Budd and others), 9.1 in 1964 by Bob Hayes and currently to 8.9.

Many factors let to the improvement through the years. Performances that occurred before 1948 were run without starting blocks on rather poor (by today's standards), unresilient tracks. Clearly, starting blocks, light-weight shoes, composition track surfaces, new starting techniques, and modern training programs have resulted in improved times from early track and field history.

An improvement of only 0.9 seconds in 93 years adds fuel to the theory of "innate ability as the main factor" at first glance. In fact, the high school record of 9.4 by Jesse Owens in 1933 stood for 34 years until Bill Gaines ran a 9.3 in 1967. Thirty-four years passed before the record was lowered 0.1 second—a tribute to the super-sprinter, Jesse Owens. With a closer look, one finds that 0.9 seconds is an improvement of slightly more than 9 percent. A 9 per cent improvement over the present one mile record would require approximately a 3:30 (four 52.5 second quarters). This will be no easy task for runners of the next 93 years, nor will it be easy to reduce the current 100-yard dash record of 8.9 to 8.1.

The fact remains that times have improved and records are being broken and rebroken, occasionally by the same individual. Individuals have also improved as much as 6/10 of a second in the 40-yard dash.

Describing The Sprinter

Body Type

There is no perfect body design for sprinting. Any one of the numerous body types and differences in height, weight and length of levers may prove effective. Although times recorded in the sprint events have improved in Olympic competition, height and weight do not appear to be factors. Present day Olympic athletes are heavier and taller than those of 30 years ago; however, they are geometrically no different from those of the past.

There is, then, no automatic additional strength and power available because of height or weight.

Heredity

Obviously, genetic laws affect the transmission of desirable or undesirable traits for sprinting much the same as in other traits. The determination of the directions for human development are transmitted through a parent's gametes, egg and sperm in the form of gigantic molecules called deoxyribonucleic acid (DNA). DNA controls development and rules body chemistry, shape and identity. Every single cell in the body contains the same DNA molecule that the zygote contained in the first place. There is much to be discovered about DNA molecules but it is safe to assume that, at birth, the game plan for development cannot be significantly altered. Both good and bad genes are present and will be reproduced with the daughter cells inheriting the whole genotype of the parent cell.

Although heredity deals the cards, environment plays the hand and strongly influences one's athletic outcome. In terms of inheriting the tendency to be a fast runner, studies of fathers' and sons' performance in the 100-yd dash correlated moderately; whereas the broad jump correlated highly. Numerous studies of identical twins also strongly suggest that there is an advantage to being the offspring of athletic parents. Regardless of your genetic make-up, you can improve your speed in short distances with proper training.

Fast- and Slow-Twitch Muscle Fiber. A single motor nerve (motoneuron) has numerous branches that enter a muscle to innervate many fibers. A motor nerve plus all the muscle fibers it innervates is referred to as a *motor unit.* With the stimulation of the motoneuron, all muscle fibers within that unit contract synchronously. A large unit consisting of many muscle fibers produces a strong contraction, while a small unit with only a few muscle fibers produces a weak contraction. Depending upon the activity, small or large motor units are stimulated to produce delicate movements such as typing or vigorous movements such as sprinting.

Motor units consist of fibers of one specific type such as *fast-twitch* (high force and high fatigue) and *slow-twitch* (low tension and fatigue resistant). Fast-twitch units contract nearly three times faster than slow-twitch units because of the increased size of individual fibers, a larger motoneuron unit (the nerve impulse is transmitted along the axon faster), and a greater number of fibers. Sarcoplasm is more abundant in some muscle fibers and contains pigment granules giving it a reddish appearance (slow-twitch or red muscle) while in others it is less abundant and muscle fibers are rather pale (fast-twitch or white muscle). The presence of different fiber types correlates with usage. Chicken muscle fiber, for example, varies greatly from breast to legs. A chicken's leg muscle fiber is dark (red) because most of the work there is slow and repetitious. The breast muscle (white) enables the chicken to make its occasional, often fear-induced flights, which require tremendous, rapid thrusts of the wings. The breast muscle fibers (white) contract rapidly and also fatigue quickly as do fast-twitch fiber in humans.

A high percentage of fast-twitch fiber in the motor units involved in sprinting enables you to sprint faster than a person who was born with a preponderance of slow-twitch fiber. Slow-twitch fiber is more suitable for endurance activities such as cross country and marathon running. During exercise such as distance running, distance swimming or cycling, motor units of slow-twitch fibers are selectively recruited. For the rapid, powerful movements of sprinting, fast-twitch fibers take preference. The same fast-twitch fibers fire over and over again and are easily fatigued in 6-10 seconds. Slow-twitch fibers fire asynchronously, which provides a built-in rest period and allows the exercise bout to continue for a long time without fatigue.

Determining your fast-twitch fiber count in the muscles involved in sprinting is difficult without a muscle biopsy (removing a small amount of tissue from various muscle groups). A noticeable lack of rapid muscle contraction in the legs during the sprinting action is a fairly reliable indicator of minimum fast-twitch fiber. Everyone (boys and girls) is born with both fast (white) and slow (red) twitch fibers. The variation of white and red fiber is very large in men. Fiber type also varies from muscle to muscle. It is possible to have many fast-twitch fiber in the legs and very little in the arms—to be able to contract the leg muscles rapidly and the arm muscles only moderately fast. Studies of fiber type of sprinters show a preponderance of fast-twitch motor units, distance runners show mostly slow-twitch units, and middle-distance runners approximately equal percentages of both types (see Table 1.1).

Type of Activity	Approximate Percentage of Fast-Twitch Fiber	
	Men	Women
Speed-type Activities:		
Sprinters (100-200-meters)	48-80%	72-75%
Ice Hockey Players	44-62%	—
Shot-putters, Discus Throwers	50-88%	45-52%
Endurance-type Activities:		
Cross Country Skiers	25-45%	25-50%
Cyclists	25-50%	35-65%
800-Meter Runners	40-64%	25-55%
Untrained Individuals	25-62%	25-72%

Table 1.1. Approximate percentage of fast-twitch fiber in speed and endurance-type athletes.

Changing slow-twitch to fast-twitch fiber is possible with specific training in sprint and strength programs. Research shows that the training may actually convert slow-twitch to fast-twitch fibers. In addition, some fast-twitch units become almost as fatigue-resistant as the slow-twitch units with endurance training. The altering of these motor units in the muscles involved in sprinting will result in faster muscle contraction, faster steps per second, and a faster 40-yard dash time. Programs designed to increase the percentage of fast-twitch fibers include a combination of strength/power training (weights, plyometrics) and sprint-assisted programs (towing, treadmill sprinting, downhill sprinting). Certainly, it is to your benefit to be born with fast-twitch dominance; however, if you are not, it is still possible to greatly increase your speed in the 40-yard dash. No one has to be destined to a sports career of slow movement in short distances. Since very few athletes ever reach their maximum personal potential, improvement is certain to occur.

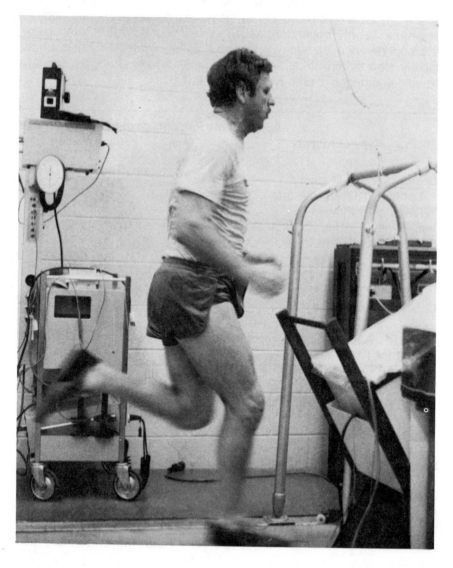

Age and Sprinting

Most champion sprinters have been under 25 years of age. Unfortunately, in the United States there has been little incentive to remain an active sprinter after the college years. Professional football, baseball, basketball, and ice hockey players maintain their speed well into their 30's. There is no physical reason for speed to diminish unless you stop training, lose considerable strength and power in the leg muscles, or gain considerable body weight and fat.

Body Fat

Resistance to rapid contraction within the muscle is provided by deposits of fat. Fat accumulates between bundles of muscle fibers and hinders their action. A reduction in total fat would also reduce these deposits. For optimum results in sprinting short distances, an athlete should possess body fat of less than 10 percent of body weight. Too much fat also provides useless weight that must be propelled through the air, thus reducing speed. Body fat can easily be estimated through the use of skinfold calipers (see Appendix B).

Racial Comparisons

Black athletes (male and female) not only tend to dominate sprint events in track and field, they are also represented above their population proportion in sports and positions where superior speed and power in short distances is important (football cornerbacks, split ends, and running backs; basketball and baseball players). There are some physical differences between whites and blacks that have implications for superior speed:
- A highly conditioned black athlete has about 38 per cent less fat than a white athlete.
- Blacks have longer legs and arms than whites.
- Blacks are significantly more muscular than whites.
- Blacks are significantly faster in knee-jerk or patellar tendon reflex than whites.
- Blacks have a higher gastrocnemius insertion (calf muscle) than whites. The high number of black college and professional athletes with superior speed in short distances leads one to wonder whether some of these physical differences aren't extremely important.

There is no reason for speed to greatly diminish with age unless your conditioning level decreases or weight gain occurs.

Circulatory Characteristics

An inverse relationship exists between speed of muscular contraction, sprinting speed and size of various animal species. A relationship also exists among the animal species between normal and maximal heart rates and speed in short distances. One elaborate study was undertaken in conjunction with the author to determine the maximum heart rate (during vigorous activity) and speed of movement of various animals. Since it is nearly impossible to consider all variables affecting these two aspects in animals, speed and heart rates were approximate with accuracy fairly high. Several findings are worthy of mention:

• The smaller the animal, the faster the heart rate.
• The greater the maximal heart rate, the faster the maximum speed of movement.
• While some animals can increase their resting heart rate four- or five-fold, man is capable of increasing heart rate only three to four times his resting pace.

Sprinters have higher resting heart rates than distance runners. Training for races of one mile to the marathon gradually reduces resting heart rates as the efficiency of the trained heart improves.

Summary

You can improve your speed in short distances such as the 40-yard dash regardless of your body type (short, tall, medium height, stocky or thin), genetic makeup, age, race, or maximum heart rate by following the proper training program. Heredity does place some restrictions on your maximum potential for improvement through the presence or absence of fast-twitch muscle fibers (white muscle) in the muscles involved in sprinting. However, a portion of slow-twitch motor units (red muscle) can be transformed to fast-twitch units through training. Research also shows that high caliber sprinters and ice hockey players possess considerably more fast-twitch fiber and less slow-twitch fiber than athletes in endurance activities such as cross country skiing and long distance running. Too much body fat also impairs rapid muscle contraction, provides useless weight for the body to move, and hinders speed of movement.

2
THE ATTACK PLAN: HOW TO DESIGN A COMPLETE PROGRAM

There is no magic formula that will make you a faster runner. Speed improvement is complicated and involves an individualized approach that identifies your specific strengths and weaknesses through careful testing, identifies the factors that are critical to your sport and position, and identifies the training programs needed to improve your 40-yard dash time. Inadequate leg strength, for example, may limit the speed of some athletes; lack of explosive power, fast muscle contraction or improper stride length may restrict others. Many athletes will have a combination of several areas needing improvement. The key is to find your specific weaknesses, then do something about them. This chapter draws from more than 375 research studies and the author's experience with more than 1500 athletes who participated in his SPEED CAMPS to present a comprehensive, individualized attack plan for the athlete in any sport who is dedicated to becoming a faster runner in short distances.

What Research Says

Before proceeding to an attack plan it is important to examine recent findings in key areas. A summary of research findings provides valuable insight into a thorough approach to speed improvement.

Anaerobic Training
(Conditioning for Sprinting Short Distances)

- Improved conditioning through the use of anaerobic training, such as short sprints, has little effect on 40-yard dash time. A high anaerobic conditioning level will, however, allow you to make repeated sprints in a contest with little slowing due to fatigue.

Body Fat and Speed

- Excess body fat restricts speed of movement in short distances by interfering with muscle fiber contraction and by adding useless weight that must be moved at high speed.

Ergogenic Aids and Speed

- Alkalis could logically be expected to aid performance in sports by reducing elevated blood acid accumulation; however, neither performance nor speed are affected.
- Benzedrine (a stimulant) is a dangerous drug capable of producing addiction, insomnia, and circulatory collapse. It has no effect upon speed.
- Ultraviolet rays have been shown to improve sprinting speed, although the exact physiological basis is not well understood.
- For some individuals, use of tobacco has a negative affect on speed in short distances.
- Caffeine, taken in various forms, has no affect on sprinting speed.
- Hormones and other steroids appear to raise fitness levels and cause strength and weight gain; they do not alter speed of movement.
- Breathing oxygen prior to sprinting does not improve 40-yard dash times.
- Phosphates (double the daily intake) appear to improve work capacity and expedite recovery following exercise; however, there is no evidence of improved speed.

Explosive Power, Strength, and Speed

- The ability to propel a stationary body into rapid movement (sprinting) requires both strength and power. An athlete may be extremely strong, yet lack explosive power and be incapable of sprinting a fast 40-yard dash. A number of training programs have been successful in bridging the gap between strength and power to improve speed.

For explosive movement, strength and power are important in most sports.

- The speed of muscle contraction can be improved with proper training.
- Speed in short distances can be improved through strength/power training.

Fast-Twitch and Slow-Twitch Fiber

- Everyone is born with both fast-twitch (white) and slow-twitch (red) muscle fiber in various parts of the body.
- It is possible to have considerable fast-twitch fiber in the leg muscles and little fast-twitch fiber in arms; i.e., to be slow moving in the arms and fast moving in the legs.
- A preponderance of fast-twitch fiber in the leg muscles is best suited for sprinting, whereas a preponderance of slow-twitch fiber is more suitable for cross country and marathon running.

Flexibility and Speed

- Ballistic (bouncing hard at the extreme range of motion) and static (applying steady pressure at the extreme range of motion without bouncing) flexibility exercises are both effective means of improving the flexibility of various joints. Static exercises are less likely to result in muscle injury or soreness.
- Increased flexibility in the ankles, hips and shoulders may help improve speed in short distances for some individuals who tend to understride because of inflexibility.

Reaction Time and Speed

- Good sprinters possess better reaction time (RT) than poor sprinters.
- RT can be improved with proper training.
- RT is a factor which affects movement time less as distance increases.
  For the short bursts of speed under 40 yards, RT is a key factor, capable of affecting total movement time by 7-24 per cent.

Stride and Speed

- Speed can be improved by increasing stride length and maintaining the same stride rate (steps per second).
- Increased stride length requires additional strength, power and flexibility. Of these three, strength and power are far more important.
- Sprinting is merely a series of jumps from one foot to the other; stride

length is increased by increasing the power of the pushoff and jumping farther.
- Stride should be lengthened in conjunction with continuous form analysis to detect possible slowing due to the introduction of a resistance phase by the foot touching the ground ahead of the center of gravity.

Stride Rate (steps per second) and Speed

- Speed can be improved by increasing stride rate and maintaining the same stride length.
- Stride rate can be increased with proper training.
- "Towing" using the Sprint Master to force you to run at speeds faster than would otherwise be possible has improved stride rate and 40-yard dash time by as much as 4/10 of a second.
- Combined downhill-uphill sprinting has been shown to force runners to take more steps per second than flat surface running.
- High speed treadmill training (speeds up to an 8.0 second 100-yard dash) improves stride rate and speed in short distances.

Training Programs

- Starting ability, acceleration, stride rate, stride length, and anaerobic conditioning can all be improved through the use of specific training programs.

Analysis of a
100-Yard Dash

Another valuable aid in identifying what factors are important for you is a thorough analysis of a 100-yard dash. For team sport athletes who accelerate to maximum speed occasionally from a stationary position and, more frequently, from a moderate speed jog, it identifies the attack points that will have the most influence on improving speed for your sport.

Acceleration, maintaining maximum velocity and deceleration vary among individuals. Superior sprinters will reach maximum speed sooner, hold maximum speed for a longer distance, and slow down less than average or less conditioned athletes.

Figure 2.1 indicates the factors involved in a 100-yard dash and their approximate point of entry for the well conditioned athlete. *Reaction to the Stimulus* is important in providing a quick muscular movement forward. *Explosive Power* or a forceful push-off combines with *Reaction* for what may be the key phase of the race—the first 2-4 yards. *Acceleration* to maximum speed occurs at different rates and is generally attained at or slightly before the 60-yard mark. *Stride Length* and *Stride Rate* now become the limiting factors for the next 15-20 yards and determine maximum speed (mph). *Anaerobic Capacity* (muscular endurance) controls the degree of slowing in the final portion of the race.

Figure 2.1. Distance of Entry for Factors Affecting the 100-Yard Dash

Factor	0 10 20 30 40 50 60 70 80 90 100	Major Role
Reaction to Gun	▉ 0.10 sec	Response to Gun
Explosive Power (Departure from blocks)	▉ 0.5 sec	Block Clearance
Accelerating Power	▉▉▉▉▉▉	Reaching Max. Speed
Stride Length/Rate	▉▉	Maximum Speed
Anaerobic Capacity	▉▉	Holding maximum, minimizing slowing

It is interesting to note that maximum speed involves only a small portion of the race (15-20 yards), a slowing effect a similar portion (10-15 yards), and acceleration the main portion (45-60 yards). Inferior reaction time, a poor start, and poor driving power can cause a runner to lose the race in the first 2-4 yards. Poor acceleration most certainly will affect the outcome of the race. An inefficient stride length and rate will affect maximum speed. And, finally, poor conditioning or low anaerobic conditioning will cause you to be overtaken late in the race.

For the team sport athlete who rarely sprints more than 40 yards and generally accelerates to full speed from a one-half to three-quarter speed pace (occasionally from a standstill), explosive power, stride length, and stride rate are important. When accelerating to full speed in this manner, maximum speed can be reached in approximately 20-30 yards.

Sprinting Strategy. For the track athlete, knowledge of the limiting factors at various stages allows one to speculate on a strategy over the racing distance that should yield maximum efficiency. Although the use of strategy is limited, a basic pattern of emphasis is necessary and the course of events is fairly predictable. It is as follows:

Start-30 Yards . . . .Rapid acceleration to 95% of maximum speed, with the greatest acceleration occuring during the first 15 yards. Considerable forward lean.

30-60 Yards . . . . . .Gradual acceleration to maximum speed and relaxed sprinting characterized by a lessening of tension at about 60 yards prior to the point where fatigue begins to hinder performance. Relatively no forward lean.

60-85 Yards . . . . . .Constant speed. Maintain but do not try to increase speed. "Fighting" to increase speed can induce rapid fatigue, disrupt smoothness of form, and cause slowing. Coasting and relaxation are not characterized by a change in form. Mastery of proper relaxation prevents speed loss and undue tightening in the final 10-15 yards.

85-100 Yards . . . . .Slight slowing effect occurs, depending upon your conditioning level. Top speed striding continues to a point 4-5 yards beyond the finish line with no body position changes. A lunge or jump at the tape, although used by some champion sprinters, may have a slowing effect.

The Major Attack Points

The preceding discussion helps to identify the major attack points to be used in speed improvement. At first glance, one might conclude that a sprinter can only take a longer or faster step. Obviously these two aspects affect a small portion of the racing distance for the 100-yard sprinter. For the team sport athlete, however, these aspects are much more critical. The major attack points for athletes in team sports are:

- RT and Improved Starting Ability
- Acceleration to Maximum Speed
- Stride Length
- Stride Rate
- Anaerobic Conditioning

At this point in your planning, the major areas of attack have been identified. It has also been established that each of these areas can be improved. You are now ready to start your diagnosis and prepare your individualized program.

Getting Started

Stop and analyze your sport and speciality from the information in Table 2.1. Identify the attack points most critical to your activity.

TABLE 2.1
Speed Improvement Attack Areas for Various Sports

Sport	Attack Areas By Priority	Comment
Football, Soccer, Rugby, Lacrosse	1. Acceleration 2. Stride rate 3. Stride length 4. Starting ability 5. Anaerobic conditioning	You run faster in the open field at top speed only by taking faster and/or longer steps. Anaerobic conditioning is important only to prevent you from slowing down after repeated short sprints.
Baseball	1. Starting ability 2. Acceleration 3. Stride rate 4. Stride length	A baseball player will not approach maximum speed unless he hits a triple or inside-the-park home run. Starting ability and acceleration should receive the most emphasis.
Basketball, Tennis, Handball, Racquetball, Squash	1. Acceleration 2. Stride rate 3. Anaerobic conditioning 4. Stride length 5. Starting ability	Most explosive action occurs after some slight movement has taken place (a jog, a bounce, or sideward movement). Maximum speed is never reached. Acceleration, stride rate and anaerobic capacity should receive primary emphasis.
Track Sprinting	1. Starting ability 2. Acceleration 3. Stride rate 4. Stride length 5. Anaerobic capacity	A 100- or 220-yard-dash sprinter must work in all five attack areas. Starting ability, acceleration, stride rate and stride length are most important.

Test Yourself. Now that you are aware of the critical attack areas for your sport, it is important to identify any physical weaknesses that may be keeping you from sprinting a faster 40-yard dash.

Example: George Byers, age 19, is a 6' 190 pound halfback on the football team. His test scores were:

Dynamic Leg Strength	= 380 lbs.	Low (not 2½ X body weight)
40-yd. Dash (stationary start)	= 4.6	Excellent
100-yd. Dash (flying start)	= 10.0	Anaerobic conditioning level is low (440 time should be no more than 5 times the 100-yd. time)
440-yd. Dash (flying start)	= 52.0	
Stride Length	= 85"	Okay
Stride Rate	= 4.7 steps per minute	Okay
Right-leg Hop	= 5.8	Okay. No real difference between right- and left-leg hops
Left-leg Hop	= 5.9	
Body Fat	= 9%	Excellent
Flexibility	= 24"	Excellent

Based on these test scores, the training programs needed for a football player such as George Byers are:

Attack Areas for Football	Training Programs Needed
1. Acceleration	Sprint-assisted Training
2. Stride Rate	Sprint-assisted Training
3. Stride Length	Weight Training, Plyometrics
4. Starting Ability	Form Training
5. Anaerobic Capacity	Interval Sprint Training

Test Weakness Areas	Training Program to Estimate Weakness
1. Leg Strength	Weight Training/Plyometrics
2. Anaerobic Conditioning	Interval Sprint Training/Hollow Sprints

Table 2.2 Test Evaluation And Standards

Test	Instrument	Purpose	Minimum Standard
40-Yd. Dash (Stationary and Flying Start)	Stop Watches (3)	To provide baseline data determining improvement	Depends upon your sport and position.
Leg Strength:			
Static	Dynamometer	Both tests of leg strength are used to determine whether your strength/weight ratio is adequate	Reading in pounds should equal 6 X your body weight
or Dynamic	Leg Press Station on Nautilus or Universal Gym		Leg press should equal 2½-3 X your body weight
Flexibility	Bench, Yard Stick	To determine whether your trunk flexion is adequate	Minimum of 20"
Anaerobic Endurance:			
440-Yd. Dash/ 100-Yd. Dash	Stop Watch	To determine whether condition is high enough to prevent slowing after repeated short sprints	440-yard dash time should be no more than 5 times your 100-yd. time
Stride Length:	Tape Measure, Track with smooth surface	To determine whether you are using your maximum stride length	16 and under boys (1.14 X height plus or minus 4"); 17 and over boys (1.265 X height); girls (1.15 X height)
Body Fat	Skinfold Calipers	To determine whether excess body fat exists	Less than 10% fat for males and 13-15% for females
Power:			
One-legged 40-yd. hop	Stop Watch	To determine whether both legs are providing equal power	The time for the left and right leg hop should be similar (within 3/10 of a second).

Interpretation	Your Personal Test Scores	Training Program If Weakness Exists
See Appendix D for interpretation; Strive for 4.5 - 5.0 minimum time with stationary start	Stationary Start = ___ Flying Start = ___	
A 170-lb.athlete should be capable of a score of 1,020 pounds	Weight X 6 = ___ Static Strength = ___ Weakness: ___ no ___ yes	Weight Training, Plyometrics
A 170-lb. athlete should be capable of a score of 425-510 pounds	Weight X 2½ = ___ Dynamic Strength = ___ Weakness: ___ no ___ yes	Weight Training, Plyometrics
From a sitting position, knees locked, you should be able to reach to the 20" mark on the yard stick	Trunk Flexion = ___ Weakness: ___ no ___ yes	Flexibility or Stretching Exercises
An athlete who can sprint 100yds. in 11.0 should complete the 440-yd.dash in 55.0 seconds	100-yd time = ___ 100-yd time X 5 = ___ 440-yd time = ___ Weakness: ___ no ___ yes	Anaerobic Training: Hollow Springs, Pick-up Sprints, Interval Sprint Training
The ideal stride for a 15 year old 5'9" boy is 1.14 X 69 or 79" ± 4" or 73-83"	Height (inches) = ___ X height = ___ Stride Length = ___ Weakness: ___ no ___ yes	Stride Training: Weight training, Plyometrics, Sprint-assisted Training, Form Training
Percent of body fat is easily determined from the chart in Appen. B	Per cent body fat = ___ More than 10% (men) More than 15% (women)	Weight reduction through diet and exercise. Consult physician
With a right foot hop of 5.3, the left foot hop should be no slower than 5.6.	R-leg hop = ___ L-leg hop = ___ Difference = ___ Weakness: ___ no ___ yes	Plyometric Training

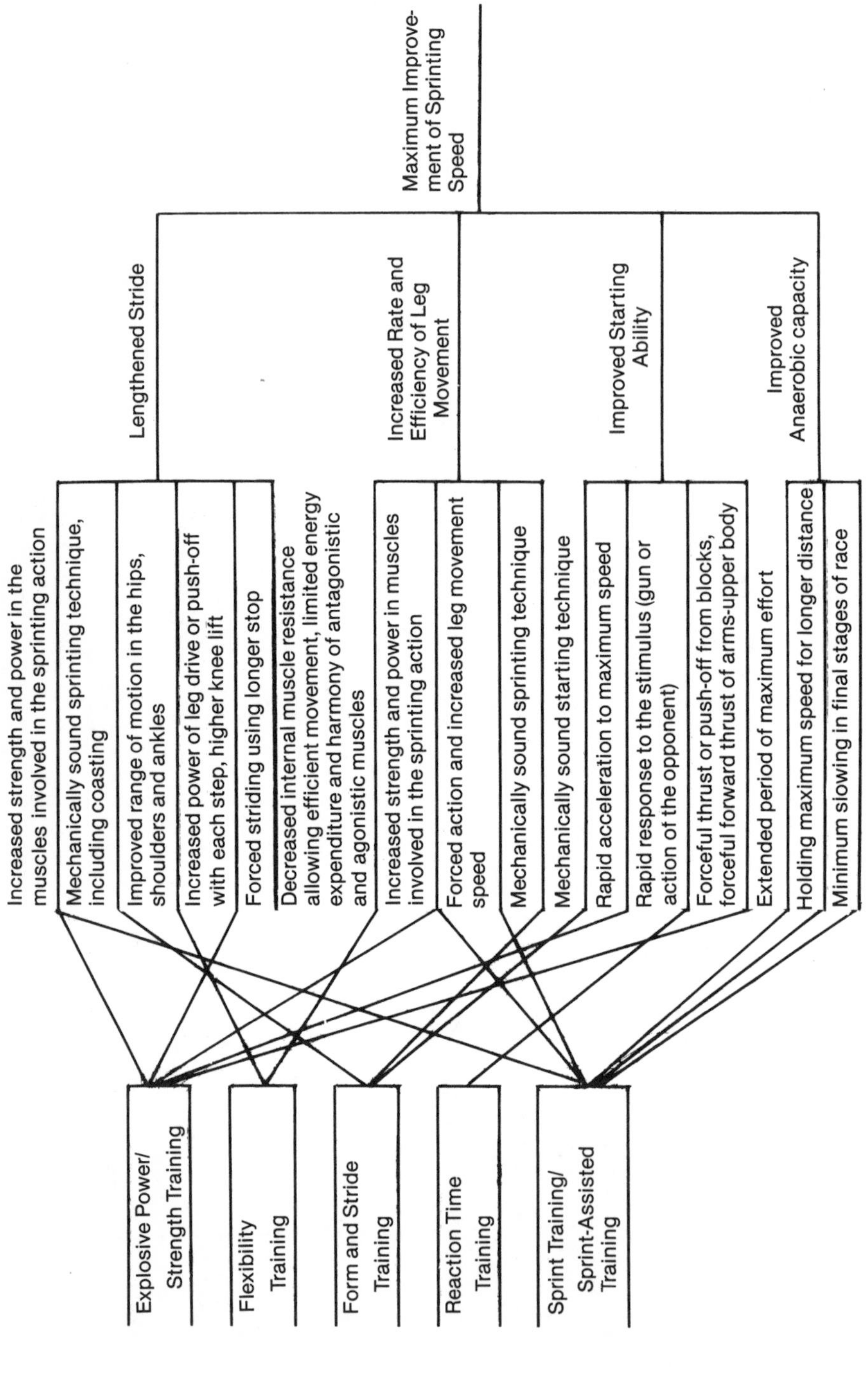

Figure 2.2 Maximum improvement of sprinting speed through specialized training programs.

Study Table 2.2 carefully before testing yourself in each of the areas. The details of test administration for each item are described in Appendices A and B. Record your scores in the last column to the right of the table and indicate whether you meet the minimum standard.

From the information you have available, list your weakness areas and the major attack areas by priority below. Using Figure 2.2 as a guide, list the specific training programs needed to improve these attack areas. Now list the training programs that are designed to eliminate any test weaknesses you have identified.

Attack Areas for your Sport
  (From Table 2.1)
1.
2.
3.
4.
5.

Training Programs Needed
  (From Figure 2.2)
1.
2.
3.
4.
5.

Test Weakness Areas

  (From Table 2.2)
1.
2.
3.
4.
5.

Training Programs to Correct Weakness
  (From Figure 2.2)
1.
2.
3.
4.
5.

Electronic testing in the 40-yard dash

Summary

It is obvious that for maximum improvement of sprinting speed a number of specialized training programs must be used. As shown in Figure 2.2, speed in short distances is improved through an increase in the length of the stride, an increase in the rate and efficiency of leg movement per second (stride rate), improved starting ability and acceleration, and improved anaerobic capacity. To plan your personalized program and identify the factors that are important to you, follow these steps:

- Test yourself in the 40-yard dash (stationary and flying start), 100-yard and 440-yard dash (flying start), leg strength, stride length, stride rate, body fat, and one-legged hops.
- Determine your weakness areas from the test interpretation column in Table 2.2.
- Identify the key speed factors for your sport and position from Table 2.1.
- Identify the training programs from Figure 2.2 that are designed to alter these factors.
- Read on and learn how to use the training programs discussed in Section II that will eliminate your weaknesses and improve your 40-yard dash time.

3

STRIDE LENGTH: HOW TO TAKE LONGER STEPS

Your maximum speed (mph rate when you are sprinting at full throttle) is determined by the length of your stride and your stride rate. For animals and humans of all sizes, maximum speed has little to do with the length of the legs. A long stride from longer legs does not guarantee faster movement rates; nor do shorter legs condemn you to slower movement rates. Short strides move more rapidly (faster stride rate) and cover as much ground as long strides and fewer steps per second. Your maximum speed then is regulated by both stride length and stride rate. To improve speed, an increase in one or both of these areas must occur without a comparable reduction in the other. In other words, you can sprint faster by taking longer steps without changing the number of steps you take per second, by taking faster steps without shortening your stride length, or by taking both longer and faster steps. This chapter helps you determine your ideal stride length and provides specific procedures to follow to lengthen your stride without reducing your stride rate.

Determining, Evaluating And Improving Your Stride Length

Your first task is to measure your exact stride length during maximum sprinting speed on a track (see Appendix A). Two markers are placed 25 yards apart on a cinder track or other soft surface that will leave a foot imprint. You should now move back approximately 50 yards from the first mark. After a thorough warmup period, begin running from this point, accelerate to maximum speed just prior to reaching the 25-yard area where you have smoothed out the surface, and sprint through this 25-yard area. With a tape measure, determine the exact length of two separate strides from the *tip of the rear toe to the tip of the front toe.* Use the average of these two measures as an indicator of your stride length.

Finish of a 40-yard dash between two individuals with the same stride rate and a stride length difference of 6 inches.

Depending upon the caliber of the sprinter studied, average maximum stride length's for top male sprinters are reported as 1.14 X height (plus or minus 4 inches), 1.24 X height, and 1.265 X height. Younger male athletes (16 and under) should use the lower value of 1.14 and older athletes the 1.265 value. The faster sprinters take longer strides and may have stride length of more than 8 feet. In controlled studies of female sprinters from various countries (100-meter times of 11.0 to 12.4 seconds), the average stride length was 1.15 X height and 2.16 times leg length. Since exact height is easier to measure than leg length (measured from the inside of the groin to the bottom of the heel), the 1.15 measure is commonly used.

  Example: Tom Hughes, age 18, 6'0"
       Optimal stride = 1.265 X 72" or 91 inches
       Lynne Rose, age 19, 5'9"
       Optimal Stride = 1.15 X 69" or 79 inches

If the stride length of Tom or Lynne is not within PLUS OR MINUS 4 inches (Tom—87-95, Lynne—75-84), stride work is indicated. These ranges also provide guidance in terms of how much stride can be lengthened without overstriding, which will hinder speed in short distances. Depending upon your test results and comparison with these suggested guidelines, one of several things may be indicated:

- Stride lengthening—for both Tom and Lynne, strides can be lengthened up to a maximum of 95 and 84 inches even if their measured strides fall within acceptable ranges.
- Stride shortening—values outside these suggested ranges may indicate the need to decrease stride length since "overstriding" hinders speed. Before attempting to shorten your stride, apply the second formula involving leg length (2.16 X leg length). Some individuals tend to have longer legs and shorter upper bodies, which distorts formulas using height. It would also be helpful to ask a coach to observe your sprinting style to determine whether your foot is actually contacting the ground surface ahead of your center of gravity (overstriding). A coach can kneel and observe as you sprint through the 25-yard area.
- No change—most runners seem to be able to find their ideal stride length. Some coaches feel that if you are within the ranges and are sprinting in a comfortable and relaxed manner, it may be best to avoid training to increase stride length. On the other hand, unless you have utilized stride lengthening techniques, it is doubtful that you have reached the maximum stride that still will not slow down your rate of leg movement per second. Most athletes can improve their 40-yard dash time by lengthening their stride.

Inches Make a Difference

Table 3.1 shows the importance of lengthening your stride by six inches without altering the stride rate of 4 steps per second. An increase in stride length of six inches improves speed by two feet per second. Every second, you are now covering two additional feet; in 10 seconds, you are covering 20 additional feet or nearly seven yards. Depending upon your original time, such a change would reduce 100-yard dash time by 0.5 to 0.9 of a second and your 40-yard dash time by 0.3 to 0.5 of a second. A 40-yard dash change from 5.0 to 4.6 is a very large improvement.

How to Increase Your Stride Length

Stride length is dependent upon several factors:
- Sprinting form
- Leg and ankle strength

- The flexibility of the hip and ankle joints
- The length of levers, which obviously cannot be changed.

Examples of excellent trunk and ankle flexibility for sprinting.

Sprinting Form. Form very definitely affects your stride length. In terms of form, the length of your stride is composed of the sum of three separate distances:
- The distance from the center of gravity to the toe of the take-off foot at the instant it leaves the ground. This factor is controlled mainly by the length of the legs and the flexibility of the hip joint.
- The horizontal distance that the center of gravity travels while you are in the air. This factor is controlled by the speed, angle, height of release, and air resistance.
- The horizontal distance that the toe of the lead foot is forward of the center of gravity at the instant of landing.

Table 3.1. Stride length increase and its effect on 40-yard dash time with a flying start.

	Stride Length		Stride Rate		Feet per Second	Approximate 40-yd. Time
Original Speed	6 Feet	X	4.0 steps-per-second	=	24 feet per second	5.0
New Speed	6'6"	X	4.0 steps-per-second	=	26.4 feet per second	4.6

These three factors are "form-related" and appear complicated. Actually, the main concern is to contact the ground with your center of gravity just ahead of the lead foot (contact foot). If the center of gravity is behind the lead foot at contact, body weight is also behind you and a slowing effect takes place. Although you can increase your stride length by placing the forward foot ahead of the body's center of gravity (overstriding), you will not improve your 40-yard dash time. Chapter 11 discusses form training and suggests ways to avoid this problem. Your task is to locate your ideal stride, then focus on other ways to increase it without changing the center of gravity at ground contact.

Leg and Ankle Strength/Power. Power is by far the most important factor in increasing stride length. Sprinting is merely a series of controlled jumps from one foot to the other that keep the center of gravity over the lead foot each time it contacts the ground. You improve stride length by pushing off with more force and jumping further. To improve the force of the pushoff you must strengthen the muscles of the lower legs, ankles and feet through weight training (Chapter 8) and Plyometric Training (Chapter 9).

Hip and Ankle Flexibility. Flexibility may be a factor for some athletes who are unable to "stretch" out during maximum speed, thus preventing them from taking their ideal stride. Complete the sit-and-reach test described in Appendix B to determine your trunk flexibility. Proper use of the flexibility exercises described in Chapter 6 as a part of your regular warm up routine will also improve your range of motion in both the ankle and trunk areas. Keep in mind, however, that you will increase your stride length mainly by improving the propulsive force and thrust of the leg against the ground, not by becoming highly flexible.

Summary

Speed can be improved by taking a longer step without reducing stride rate. Your first task in lengthening your stride is to measure your steps during maximum speed and compare this length to the standards provided for your height or leg length. Unless your measured stride length is at the extreme range, stride lengthening is indicated. You improve your stride length mainly by increasing the force of the push-off each time the foot strikes the ground; this is accomplished through weight training and plyometric training. Flexibility training may also be needed if you score low on the sit-and-reach test. For the inflexible athlete, increased flexibility will allow the ideal stride length to be taken without undue muscle resistance.

Form training is not likely to improve stride length unless your center of gravity is far ahead of the lead foot at ground contact. In this case, a longer stride would place the center of gravity just slightly ahead and improve speed. After you attain your optimal stride length, improving your 40-yard dash time becomes a matter of increasing stride rate (steps per second).

4

STRIDE RATE: HOW TO TAKE FASTER STEPS

Stride rate is the sum of the time for ground contact and the time you are in the air. For top sprinters, this ratio is 2:1 at the start of the race and 1:1.3—1:1.5 at maximum speed later in the race. It is determined by speed, angle, height of release and air resistance in flight. Of these, release or ground reaction forces seem most important. In other words, it is important to push-off as rapidly as possible and avoid too much height that would create wasted time in the air. A good sprinter is said to run low to the ground and be in the air 50 percent of the time and in contact with the ground the remaining 50 per cent.

In the animal world, the cheetah has been clocked at 70 mph and has reached a speed of 45 mph in 2 seconds. The cheetah and the horse both have a stride length of about 23 feet; however, the stride rate of a cheetah is 1½ times that of the horse,whose maximum speed is only 46 mph.

Top sprinters have a stride rate of about 5 steps per second (males) and 4.48 steps per second (females) with a maximum speed of about 26 mph. Females are approximately one second slower than males in the 100-yard dash due to slower stride rates. Ground reaction forces and power differences are the main cause. Children run with faster strides than adults. As height and leg length increases, stride rate decreases. The longer the legs, the more power required to move them at the same rate. Contrary to popular opinion, the long-legged, tall sprinter has no mechanical advantage over the short legged, small sprinter. Longer legs result in a longer stride but slower stride rate. It takes considerable more strength, power, and energy to move long levers through the complete cycle in sprinting than it does short levers. Fast strides in both animals and humans take great power in the legs, ankles, and buttocks.

Improving Stride Rate

In the past, the stride rate was considered an unalterable factor fixed at birth by the nervous and muscular systems' ability to produce rapid contraction and relaxation. There is now evidence to the contrary. Higher stride rates are possible in cycling (5.5—7.1 per second), towing (6.0—7.5), treadmill sprinting (6—7.3), and downhill sprinting (5—5.8) than in sprinting. The limiting factors are external (wind, surface conditions) and internal forces (strength/power ratio, muscle resistance, fat deposits between bundles of muscle fibers, and the prevalence of fast and slow-twitch fiber in the muscle involved in sprinting).

Warmup and Stride Rate

Logic supports the value of warmup for improved stride rate and speed. The increased muscle temperature, the added synovial fluid to lubricate the knee joint, the reduced internal joint and muscle resistance, the increased blood flow, the improved climate for conducting chemical activity and the fact that muscle contraction in animals is quickened by as much as 20 percent with a 2°C increase in body temperature all indicate that speed should improve. Although improvement in humans is much less dramatic and often unnoticeable, it is wise to use formal warmup (jog-stride-sprint) for 15-25 minutes prior to sprinting to prevent muscle injury and guarantee rapid contraction of the large muscle groups.

Body Fat and Stride Rate

Resistance to rapid contraction within the muscle is provided by deposits of fat. Fat accumulates between bundles of muscle fibers and hinders their action. A reduction in total body fat would also help reduce these deposits. It is beyond the scope of this book to discuss nutrition and fat reduction techniques. A sprinter should, however, possess body fat of less than 10 per cent (males) or 15 per cent (females) of body weight. Since weight charts are grossly inadequate, even as an estimate of normal body fat, the skinfold method should be used. Measurement at only one site(triceps—back of upper arm)will provide you with an estimate of your percent of body fat (see Appendix B for instructions on how to measure your body fat).

Air Resistance and Stride Rate

Air resistance takes approximately 7 to 9 per cent of a sprinter's energy even in calm weather. Air density, your projected surface area, and the square of the wind determine energy costs. A head wind will slow down a larger runner more than a smaller runner. Conversely, a tail wind will aid a larger runner more because of the larger surface area for the wind to contact. Head and tail winds will also affect stride rate by slowing or speeding up the knee lift.

Sprint-Assisted Training and Stride Rate

Stride rate can be improved in most athletes by changing a percentage of slow-twitch (red muscle) to fast-twitch (white muscle) motor units. This altering of muscle fiber type seems to occur best through strength/power training (Weight Training and Plyometrics) and sprint-assisted training (towing, treadmill sprinting, downhill sprinting, and cycling). The full extent to which this occurs is not well understood and evidence is somewhat conflicting in terms of whether a change actually occurs. Sprint-assisted training has been found to improve stride rate and speed in the 40- and 50-yard dash. Subjects in the Virginia Commonwealth University Human Performance Laboratory trained five times weekly on a high speed treadmill for six weeks while a control group was involved in a traditional sprint training program similar to those commonly used by track coaches. Both groups were pre- and post-tested in a 40-yard dash with a flying start and in stride rate (steps per second). Treadmill trained subjects sprinted at speeds 1-3 miles per hour faster than their best unaided effort on a track. Some of the faster athletes sprinted at rates equivalent to a 8.5 to 9.0 second 100-yard dash. Subjects were protected by two spotters and a suspended belt that supported the sprinter as speeds exceeded his maximum. Treadmill subjects improved their unaided 40-yard dash time by an average of 3/10 of a second. Stride rates also increased significantly. No significant improvement occurred in the control group in stride rate or 40-yard dash time.

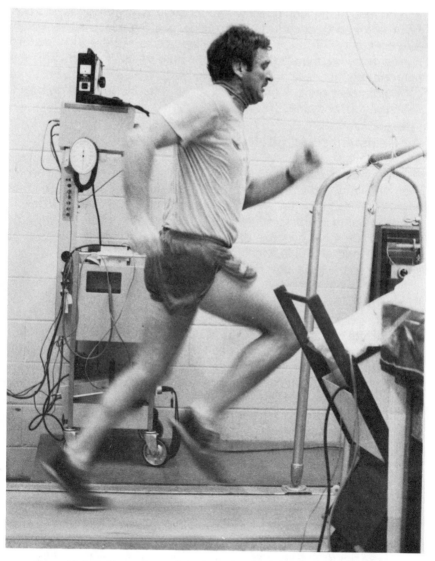

Super high stride rates can be produced on the high speed treadmill.

Towing and the combination of downhill/uphill sprinting have also increased stride rate and speed in short distances. Towing is the most practical and effective sprint-assisted method in use today. Just why there is carryover to unaided sprinting following involvement in these sprint-assisted programs is unknown. It is theorized that perhaps some of the slow-twitch motor units are being converted to fast-twitch units and that neurological patterns are established that carry-over to unaided sprinting to produce faster times. Chapter 7 describes four sprint-assisted programs and provides sample workouts for each. You should engage in one of these programs three times weekly (every other day) immediately after you have warmed up and before you become fatigued from any other phase of the workout.

Towing also produces extremely high stride rates.

Strength/Power Training and Stride Rate

Improving your strength/weight ratio (see Chapter 2, Table 2.2, Leg Strength Test) is critical to taking faster steps. For female athletes, it may be the single most important factor. It serves to improve ground reaction forces and lessen the time for ground contact without loss of pushoff power. Follow the program described in Chapter 8.

Form Training and Stride Rate

Stride rate depends upon four form-related factors:
- The speed of extension of the driving leg.
- The speed with which you bring through the recovering leg.
- The length of time you spend in the air.
- The landing position of the recovery foot relative to your center of gravity.

Chapter 11 helps you to sprint with the proper technique to enable you to take the maximum number of steps per second possible without hindering your 40-yard dash time.

Pump and Stride Training and Stride Rate

After a thorough warmup of jogging and flexibility exercises, the pump and stride method can be used to improve stride rate. Runners execute three repetitions of 50 yards by bringing the knees toward the chest as far as possible and gradually moving forward for 50 yards. One hundred high knee pumps (20 every 10 yards) should be executed. A two minute walking rest interval is used between each repetition. Runners increase the distance to 75 and 100 yards over a 3-4 week period. Major emphasis is placed on rapid knee/arm pumping and high knee lifts.

Pump and stride training — the pump and the sprint forward.

Summary

Improving stride rate requires a number of special approaches. The specific training programs include combined downhill/uphill sprinting, towing (the most practical and effective method), treadmill sprinting, strength/power training, pump and stride training, and the elimination of excess body fat. The key factor to remember is that stride rate can be increased and that even a slight change will improve your time in the 40-yard dash.

5

ANAEROBICS: HOW TO GET IN CONDITION TO SPRINT SHORT DISTANCES

The ability to sprint a short distance of 10–100 yards with limited interference from fatigue depends upon the short-term anaerobic energy system. Sports such as football, baseball, tennis, racquetball, squash, basketball and 100-yard sprinting in track rely almost exclusively on energy derived from the anaerobic system. Even athletes in soccer, rugby, lacrosse and field hockey need anaerobic training since approximately 80 per cent of the energy to perform in these sports also comes from the anaerobic system.

The anaerobic energy system can be improved to provide additional energy for repeated all-out short sprints through use of the training methods described in Section II, Chapter 10. This chapter attempts to present a simplified explanation of the anaerobic energy system and establish guidelines for you to follow that will ensure improvement. Unless the system is trained properly, you will be incapable of sprinting repeated short distances in your sport without considerable "slowing" due to fatigue. In addition, a poorly conditioned anaerobic system will cause you to slow down at the end of the distance even on the first sprint.

Anaerobic Metabolism

Anaerobic metabolism comes into action at the onset of any type of exercise as an immediate source of quick energy until circulatory and respiratory adjustments occur. Sprinting always takes place in the absence of oxygen, a condition under which the skeletal muscles can function for only a short time. The intensity and short duration of sprinting is such that respiratory and circulatory systems have no time to adapt; the oxygen requirements immediately exceed the possible oxygen uptake. Obviously, the ability to breathe in and use atmospheric oxygen is of very little importance to sprinting short distances. In fact, you could hold your breath while sprinting 40 yards and it would have absolutely no effect on your time. Any air you breathe in during a short sprint is not utilized. Consequently, you enter into what is termed "oxygen debt" (you owe the body oxygen) during the sprint. After the sprint is completed, this oxygen debt is repaid while you are resting. Study Table 5.1 carefully to

Table 5.1. Sports and Their Predominant Energy Systems

| Sport | Per cent Emphasis per Energy System | | |
| | Anaerobic | | Aerobic |
	ATP-PC and LA	LA-O_2	O_2
Baseball	80	20	0
Basketball	85	15	0
Field Hockey	60	20	20
Football	90	10	0
Ice Hockey:			
Forwards, defense	80	20	0
Goalie	95	5	0
Lacrosse:			
Goalie, defense, attack men	80	20	0
Midfielders, man-down	60	20	20
Soccer			
Goalie, wings, strikers	80	20	0
Halfbacks, link men	60	20	20
Tennis	70	20	10
Track and field			
40-220 Yards	99	1	0
440 Yards	80	15	5
Mile	20	55	25

Table 5.2. Training Methods and Their Effect on the Energy Systems

Training Method	Definition	Anaerobic ATP-PC and LA	LA-O$_2$	Aerobic O$_2$
Pick-up Sprints	Gradual increases in speed from jogging to striding to sprinting in 25-120 yd. segments	90%	5%	5%
Hollow Sprints	Two sprints interrupted by "hollow" periods of jogging or walking	85%	10%	5%
Interval Sprints	Alternate sprints of 20-300 yards followed by jogging and walking for recovery	80%	10%	10%
Jogging	Continuous running at a slow pace over a distance of 2 or more miles	0	0	100%
Sprint-assisted Training	Repeated sprints at maximum speed aided by towing, downhill, or treadmill with complete recovery between each repetition.	90%	6%	4%

identify the system supplying the energy for your sport. Your training for conditioning purposes should reflect these proportions. As you can see, the training programs shown in Table 5.2 and discussed in Chapter 10 train the anaerobic system almost proportionally to provide you with the maximum amount of quick energy and rapid utilization of that energy for your sport.

Understanding the muscle as a machine for converting chemical into mechanical energy is a complicated phase of physiology. With sufficient oxygen available (aerobic exercise such as a 5-mile run), fatigue lactates in the muscles are absent. When oxygen supplies are insufficient (anaerobic exercise such as short sprints), pyruvic acid forms from glucose and is reduced to lactic acid. This process (anaerobic glycolysis) only occurs in the absence of oxygen to produce energy-rich phosphate bonds to allow muscle contraction to continue. These quick energy stores are nearly depleted in 8 seconds of maximum effort sprinting. At this point (much sooner for the unconditioned athlete) slowing occurs due to lactic acid build-up. Improved lactic acid tolerance, increased quick energy stores, and improvement in the rate you can utilize the quick energy available (phosphagen) depends upon factors such as training, age (highest at age 20-25, decreasing slowly thereafter) and nutrition.

Anaerobic Training

With training, higher levels of blood lactate concentration can be tolerated. The well trained athlete achieves a higher concentration of lactic acid than an untrained athlete. Both physiological and psychological adaptation occurs.

The following guidelines govern anaerobic conditioning programs:
- Sprinting (up to 220 yards) is 99% anaerobic and training should reflect this percentage. Aerobic training (distance training such as slow jogging for 2-5 miles) should occupy only a small portion of your training regime. The availability of additional oxygen, as demonstrated in the previous discussion, is of no value. It is impossible for the respiratory system to use atmospheric oxygen once the gun is fired. Therefore, improved oxygen uptake can in no way improve your speed in short distances.
- Aerobic training also has no effect upon lactic acid tolerance, stride length or stride rate.
- You should avoid anaerobic and aerobic training at the same time. Two one-half hour sessions of aerobic training weekly are sufficient.
- The principle of specificity should be followed. Training occurs, in part, within the muscles themselves and training is specific in terms of lactic acid production during vigorous exercise. Thus, complete training transfer, regardless of the closeness of the activities, is not possible. Maximum work for team sport athletes must involve all-out sprints. This also facilitates the recruitment of the exact same motor units used in sprinting. In addition, fast-twitch fibers are activated by short duration, high-power work such as sprinting. Slow running will activate and train the slow-twitch fibers.
- The anaerobic system must be "overloaded" by engaging the muscles involved in sprinting in repeated maximum bursts for 5-10 seconds interspersed with 30-60 second rest intervals. Bouts of 30 seconds to one minute will cause lactic acid to reach near maximum levels and are also sound training approaches. A 3-5 minute rest interval following these longer bouts cause "lactate stacking" that produces higher lactic acid levels than you can build up in only one all-out effort. The decisive factor in lactic acid concentration is the length of the work period. At

maximum speed, distances closer to 440 yards will produce the highest lactic acid levels. Recovery time and the relationship between the rest interval and work are secondary.

- A one-minute maximum-effort sprint, followed by 3-5 minutes of rest before repeating the effort can produce high lactic acid concentrations in the blood and an arterial pH of 7.0 or lower. Repetitive 440-yard runs in less than 60 seconds, followed by a 3-5 minute rest period, are an effective technique for training the anaerobic system.

- A 30-second maximum sprint, followed by 2-4 minutes of rest before repeating the effort 2-6 times, is an excellent approach to the training of the anaerobic system for football players.

- Traditional wind sprints as used by many coaches are of little value in improving the anaerobic system unless accurate records are kept on the distance covered, the number of short sprints, and the rest interval between each sprint. Keep in mind that you must do more work each day if improvement in conditioning is to occur. It is more effective to do more work by slowly lengthening the sprint distance and shortening the rest interval between each sprint. Brief record keeping from day to day is necessary.

- Traditional calisthenics as used by many coaches at the beginning of a workout are also of little value in improving the anaerobic system. Again the body must be exposed to progressively more work each day if a training effect is to take place. This requires increasing the number of repetitions for each calisthenic exercise daily, reducing the rest interval between each exercise, and increasing the speed with which each exercise is done. Alternating leaders who direct the calisthenics with little concern for these factors will not improve anaerobic conditioning levels. In addition, it is doubtful that calisthenics, other than stretching exercises, should be used at the beginning of any workout as a conditioning technique. It is undesirable to tire an athlete in any sport at the very beginning of a workout. Fatigued athletes perform poorly in drills (timing is off), form is affected, and they are more likely to be injured in contact and high speed work. If the purpose of calisthenics is to condition the anaerobic system, they should be vigorously administered at the end of the practice session or workout. Also, the anaerobic system is best trained for sprinting short distances by actual sprint training that involves these same muscle groups, not by calisthenic movements.

- Anaerobic training requires a rather lengthy time period for full recovery. Anaerobic programs should therefore be used at the end of the workout to prevent fatigue from hindering skill training, altering timing in team sports, making you more susceptible to injury, or preventing you from taking your longest, fastest step while sprinting.

Summary

An athlete with a high level of anaerobic training will be capable of sprinting repeated short sprints with little or no slowing due to fatigue. Training must involve repetitions of actual sprinting at full speed for distances of 20–440 yards, interrupted by a controlled recovery interval of walking or jogging. A variety of sprint training methods are effective in improving anaerobic conditioning. For a discussion of the common programs that apply the training guidelines presented in this chapter, see Chapter 10.

SECTION II:
THE
TRAINING
PROGRAMS

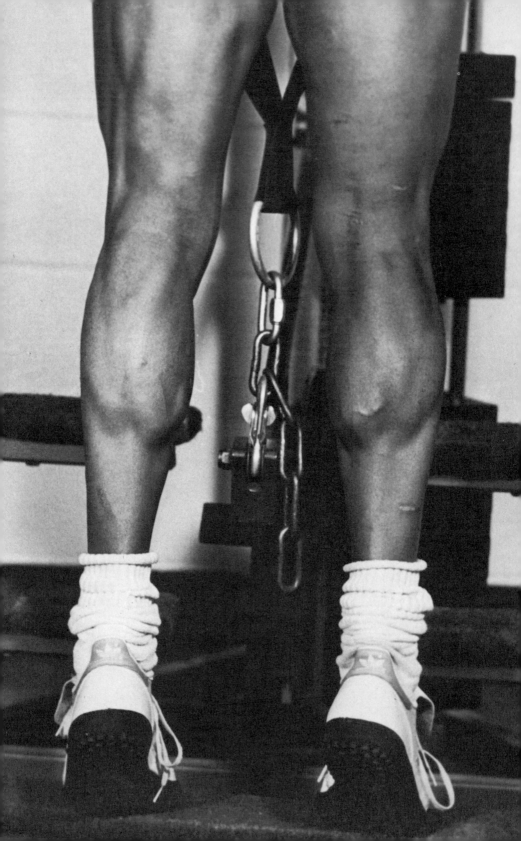

6

INTRODUCTION: PRINCIPLES OF CONDITIONING FOR SPEED IMPROVEMENT

The mere participation in an exercise program or sport is no guarantee that your conditioning level will improve. With some simple record keeping and the application of a few basic principles, however, you can make tremendous gains in your fitness level with little risk of injury or illness. This chapter discusses these conditioning principles and their application to speed improvement programs to help you get started on an effective program.

Principles of Conditioning

Work Hypertrophy

To improve your conditioning level, you must apply the *concept of work hypertrophy.* Don't let the terminology scare you. It merely means that you must do more work tomorrow (per unit of time) than you did today. Let's examine this concept further. When you begin an exercise program, you are at a certain conditioning level. Your first workout destroys muscle tissue and actually lowers this level at the workout's end. At this point, however, nature goes to work and regenerates tissue, rebuilding the body to a point higher than it was before the initial workout began. It is similar to nature's reaction to your hands after shoveling the first winter snow. Calluses form within a short time to toughen the hands in preparation for more vigorous shoveling. On the second workout day, you are equipped to perform more exercise than before and, to continue to apply this concept, you must perform more work each day so that nature again rebuilds the body beyond the level of the previous workout.

Does it sound complicated? It isn't. There are only a few things to remember in order to apply the work hypertrophy concept:

• Exercise must be intense enough to destroy tissue—nature's rebuilding process is somewhat in proportion to this intensity.
• The second, third, fourth, etc. workout must take place without too much recovery time between workouts (24-48 hours). Allowing too much time will result in a lower conditioning level.
• Enough recovery time must be allowed for rebuilding to take place. If you exercise before full recovery occurs, you defeat your purpose. Some coaches and athletes make this mistake with double training sessions. Unless one session is conditioning oriented and the other devoted to skill development with minimum exercise, the conditioning value is limited and may actually slow down physical improvement.
• Each workout should be progressively more strenuous than the previous. Think through this concept. Apply it to each of your training programs by recording daily workout sessions. Compare one workout to another. Set work goals and systematically strive to reach them.

Specificity (All Training Programs)

Training is unique to an activity or sport. In other words, football or soccer players who have just completed their seasons will find that they are not capable of meeting the physical demands of wrestling or basketball. A transitional period will be needed before maximum efficiency is reached in the new sport. In order to train the fast-twitch motor units, highly intense sprint-type exercise is needed to ensure that the same fibers will be activated that are used in sprinting short distances.

Alternate Light and Heavy Training (All Training Programs)

The body responds best to training programs that alternate light and heavy workouts. This approach reduces the risk of injury, provides several emotionally relaxing workouts each week, and allows the body time to repair fully between workouts. In other words, it helps you receive maximum benefit from your conditioning program.

Warmup (All Training Programs)

As indicated in Chapter 4, warmup is almost universally used for the purpose of improving performance, preventing muscle and joint injuries, and acquiring maximum flexibility. Research indicates that warm-up should be used for 20-25 minutes prior to activity and that only a few minutes should elapse from the completion of the warmup period until the start of the activity. Warmup will not bring about early fatigue and hinder performance.

Warmup methods fall into four categories:

Formal— Using the skill or act that will be used in competition; running before a 100-yard dash.

Informal— General warmup involving calisthenics or other unrelated exercises.

Passive— Applying heat to various body parts in numerous forms.

Overload— Simulating the activity for which warmup is being used by increasing the load or resistance, such as use of weighted boots prior to a 100-yard dash.

Each of these warmup methods has been shown to be helpful by some researchers. Formal warmup appears to be superior to informal warmup. There is little evidence to suggest the use of overload warmup as a method of improving speed in short distances.

As important as the type of warmup is its length. Muscle temperature rises in 5 minutes and continues to rise for 25-30 minutes. With inactivity, the effects drop rapidly until, after 45 minutes, additional warmup is needed. It would seem advisable to use 20-25 minutes of warmup that causes perspiration and is a progressive procedure leading to all-out effort. Find the magic combination for you and your activity, then stay with it.

Numerous investigators have reported that warmup significantly improves speed in short distances while others report no such cause-effect relationship. One-hundred-yard dash times have been reduced as much as .94 seconds following intense formal warmup. There is also some evidence that speed can be improved through the use of artificial heat. It is interesting to note that no one has ever indicated that warmup is detrimental to sprinting speed.

Warm-down (All Training Programs)

The explanation for a warm-down period at the end of a vigorous workout is quite simle. Blood returns to the heart through a system of vessels called veins. The blood is pushed along by the contraction of the heart and the "milking" action of the muscles. The veins are contracted or squeezed through muscular action which moves the blood forward against the force of gravity while valves in the veins prevent the blood from backing up. If you stop suddenly, the milking action of the muscles, which occurs only through muscular contraction, will stop; the blood return will drop quickly and may cause blood pooling in the legs (blood remains in the same area) leading to shock or deep breathing. The deep breathing then lowers the carbon dioxide levels and muscle cramps develop. These cramps may last for 24-48 hours.

You should warm down following a vigorous sprint training session. A general warm-down routine might consist of running 880 yards to one mile at a pace of two or three minutes per quarter-mile, each quarter -mile slower than the previous one. Stretching exercises can also be used as a warm-down following your strength training workout.

Flexibility Training

Stretching exercises are important in practically all team sports. For the improvement of sprinting speed, flexibility routines help to increase stride length, permit free arm movement in sprinting, limit internal muscle resistance, assist in the prevention of muscle injuries, limit energy expenditure, and improve the harmony between the antagonistic or relaxing muscles and the agonistic or contracting muscles when you are sprinting. Flexibility exercises should be performed early in the workout prior to any vigorous activity and again following the weight training session.

For the stretching exercises shown for sprinters, each static movement is held in a position of maximum flexion or extension for 30 seconds to one minute. Repeat each movement 2-5 times, with a rest interval of 15-30 seconds between each repetition.

Stretching exercises for the improvement of flexibility.

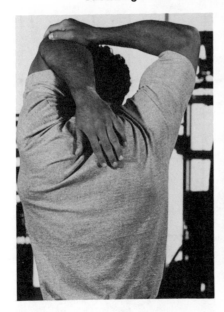

Stretching exercises (Cont.)

Stretching exercises (Cont.)

Stretching exercises (Cont.)

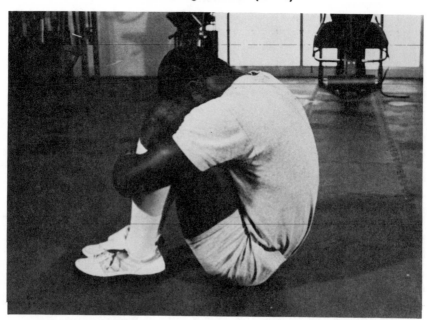

Stretching exercises (Cont.)

Order of Training Programs in a Workout

Of the many types of programs suggested for speed improvement, not all will be used in one workout. The order in which you place warmup, sprint-assisted training, form training, anaerobic training, strength training, plyometrics and warm-down in your workout, however, is very important. Table 6.1 lists the workout order for each of these programs, provides a guide to the number of times weekly each should be used, and explains the logic behind careful placement in a workout. Using a sprint-assisted method at the end of a workout when you are fatigued, for example, is completely worthless. Your leg muscles cannot contract at super-high rates; nor can you take long strides when you are fatigued. Using weight training or plyometrics at the beginning of your workout will also leave you too fatigued to benefit from any of the other items in that training session. Consult the chart to find the correct order for your workout.

Training Program	Length	Workout Order	Frequency	Explanation
Warmup (Stretching)	8-12 min.	1	Daily	Perform the flexibility exercises pictured in this chapter.
Sprint-Assisted Training	30 min.	2	Every other day	You should be completely fatigue free before using any of these programs
Form Training	10-15 min.	3	Twice weekly	You should be relatively free of fatigue during form training
Anaerobic Training	20 min.	4	Every other day	Your main objective is to exhaust the anaerobic system
Strength/Power Training	15-30 min.	5	Every other day	Always the last program in your workout since it produces extreme muscular fatigue
Plyometrics	12-15 min.	5	Every other day	Always the last program in your workout; should not be used on days that you engage in weight training
Warm-down	8-10 min.	6	Daily	Use light jogging after anaerobic training or stretching exercises after strength/power training

Table 6.1. Order of use for various training programs.

Time	Order	Program	Purpose	Comment
5-7 min.	1	Flexibility exercises	Increased range of motion Warmup effect, increased stride length	Little conditioning value, warmup prior to vigorous activity without undue fatigue, reduces injury
5-18 min.	2	Sprint training Sprint-assisted training	Stride rate/length Acceleration Anaerobic capacity	Short session while athletes are free from fatigue to work on speed factors
75 min.	3	Normal session in football, baseball, soccer basketball	Mastery of sports skills, strategy, and conditioning through game related drills	Major portion of practice session
15 min.	4	Calisthenics, running	General conditioning, anaerobic/aerobic work	Major thrust of conditioning at close of practice
10-15 min.	5	Strength/power training	Improved power, stride rate/length, acceleration	2-3 times weekly for improvement, once weekly to maintain

Table 6.2. Practice Placement of Supplementary Programs during the In-Season Period.

Practice Placement of Supplementary Programs

Supplementary programs are used in most sports. The normal practice session during the in-season period is not sufficient to develop high levels of strength, power, speed, flexibility, and anaerobic and aerobic capacity. The use of such programs create two major problems: in what order should these programs be used in a practice session, and how do these programs fit into a tight schedule? With misuse, the training effect is reduced, the practice session is less beneficial, and the chance of player injury is increased. Table 6.2 serves to present a logical order as well as demonstrate the minimal time involvement for team sport use. No athlete in any sport achieves championship caliber without using a number of supplementary programs. These programs can be used in season and out of season for more concentrated work on weakness areas.

Summary

Mere participation in a sport will not automatically take you to your maximum conditioning level. Unless some basic principles are followed, little improvement will occur. You must systematically do more work each training session, train at least every other day, alternate light and heavy days, train the specific muscle groups that are used in your sport under exactly the same conditions, and properly use a warmup and warm-down period. The order in which different programs are used in a workout is also critical. A warmup period of stretching exercises should be used at the beginning of a workout, followed by sprint-assisted training when you are fatigue-free. The skill development part of your sport (scrimmage, drills, etc.) then takes place and is followed by the conditioning phase (anaerobic training, calisthenics, strength training, plyometrics) and a brief warm-down period. It is possible to incorporate a number of these supplementary programs into the practice session in your sport during the in-season period.

7
SPRINT-ASSISTED TRAINING

Sprint-assisted programs (overspeed training) attempt to improve sprinting speed by increasing stride rate and stride length. These programs allow you to sprint at much faster speeds than you could run in flat surface, unaided sprinting. The purpose of sprint-assisted training is to force you to take longer and faster steps to carry over to unaided sprinting on an athletic field.

This chapter discusses the merits of four sprint-assisted programs and provides suggested workouts for each: towing, downhill sprinting, stationary cycling, and treadmill sprinting. You should select at least one of these programs and make it a part of your workout routine two to three times weekly.

Towing

Towing athletes behind automobiles, motor scooters and motorcycles is not a new approach to the improvement of speed. In 1956, towing was used to train Olympic medal winner Al Lawrence, who held on to a rigid bar attached to a car four times weekly for distances of 100-600 yards. In the 1960's it was successfuly used in Australia to reduce the 100-meter dash time of one subject who held on to the side of a tram car. In the U.S. a pacing machine (tow bar and handle attached to the rear bumper of a car) was used in 1961. Young runners increased their stride length considerably (average of 6") and improved their 100-yard dash time from an average of 10.5 to 9.9. In 1976, a four-station tow bar attached to an auto was used

Towing using an automobile and tow line.

to improve 40-yard dash time with a flying start. Towing has since been a regular part of our SPEED CAMPS and "overspeed" or sprint-assisted training an important part of our program to improve 40-yard dash times.

The *Dolan Sprint Master* is by far the most refined and practical method of towing athletes either on a football field or in the gymnasium. No auto, motor scooter or motorcycle is needed. The machine is precisely engineered to pull athletes at speeds faster than any human being alive can sprint without assistance. It attaches to the goal posts of a football field or to the wall of a gymnasium and provides controlled, precise, variable speed for each athlete. This practical device is very safe and eliminates the cumbersome, dangerous use of a vehicle. For a brochure and information on the purchase of a Sprint Master for you or your institution, write: Sprint Master, Box 2936, Richmond, Virginia 23235.

The Sprint Master allows you full and proper use of your arms while being towed at speeds of 5/10 to 1 second faster than your best 40-yard dash with a flying start. The following steps are used to start a sprint-assisted program with the sprint master:

l. Test yourself in the 40-yard dash with a flying start (see Appendix A).

2. Determine your approximate speed (mph) from Table 7.1.

3. Use the workout schedule shown in Table 7.2 two to three times weekly

Forty - Yard* Time	Feet Per Second	Miles Per Hour
5.08	24.32	10.58
4.89	25.49	17.38
4.70	26.66	18.18
4.51	27.83	18.98
4.32	29.00	19.77
4.13	30.18	20.58
3.94	31.35	21.38
3.75	32.52	22.17
3.56	33.70	22.98
3.37	34.87	23.98
3.18	36.04	24.46
2.99	37.21	25.14
2.88	37.90	25.82

*Flying start of 15-25 yards used; runners are in full sprinting stride when the stop watch begins.

Table 7.1 Forty-Yard Dash Time, Feet Per Second, and MPH

(every other day) immediately after your warmup or stretching routine, before you are fatigued from any other phase of your workout.

4. When you are being pulled, grasp the tow rope handles and accelerate slowly for 25-35 yards. The Sprint Master will then exert its proper pull as you reach full speed and will continue to pull you for 15-20 yards. A distance of 15-20 yards at high speed is sufficient; longer distances will produce fatigue and cause you to lose your balance.
5. Runners are taught to "let go" of the tow rope handles if balance is lost. On an athletic field, particularly in full football gear, a high speed fall and a roll is generally safe. In actual use of the Sprint Master, very few runners actually fall at any towing speed. In our 1981 Speed Camp, only one runner in 610 pulls fell on the first training session.

Week	Repetitions	Acceleration Distance	Pull Distance	Repetition Progression	Rest (Min.)	Speed of the Sprint Master
1	5-9	25-35 yds.	15-20 yds	Add 1-2 each workout	1-2	Slow at 3/4 speed to acclimate athletes
2	3-5	25-35 yds.	15-20 yds	Add 1 each workout	2	Towing at 3/10 second faster than 40-yd. time
3	5-8	25-35 yds.	15-20 yds	Add 1 each workout	3	Towing at 5/10 second faster than 40-yd. time
4	9-11	25-35 yds.	15-20 yds	Same each workout	4	Towing at 7/10 second faster than 40-yd. time
5	Retest in the 40-yard dash with a flying start and repeat the above workout beginning at week 2.					

Table 7.2 Towing program for improving speed in the 40-yard dash using the Sprint Master

6. Use the full 2-4 minutes of rest between each towing repetition. It is important to be completely fatigue-free each repetition to allow you to take a long stride and fast steps.

Sprint Master operation can be easily learned and is described precisely in the brochure. Speeds can be individually determined for each athlete and the pull can be made by the operator safely and accurately.

The Dolan Sprint Master can be attached to the gymnasium wall or the goal posts for indoor or outdoor use.

Towing using the Sprint Master.

Towing with the Sprint Master is the most effective and practical sprint-assisted program for athletes of all ages. It can be used both during the off-and in-season period on a regular basis.

Downhill Sprinting

Some experts feel that higher speeds in downhill sprinting are only imaginary. Too much slope creates a greater body lean, resulting in the driving foot contacting the ground further under the body than desirable, thereby reducing the time available for a forceful push against the surface. This would produce faster leg rates at the expense of reduced stride length. In controlled downhill training, the problem is eliminated when a slope of 2.6° or less is used. European countries have used combined downhill-uphill training with some success. In one experiment, a group of subjects training on downhill, uphill and flat surfaces improved speed significantly more than groups using only one type of surface. Other studies have demonstrated improved times in short distances following downhill sprint training programs. The key to the use of downhill sprinting as a sprint-assisted program is to locate a hill with a moderate slope of 2.6 or less. A sample program is described in Table 7.3.

Downhill sprinting with the proper slope.

Stationary Cycling

It has long been observed that individuals are capable of higher rates of leg alternation in cycling (5.5 – 7.1 per second) than in sprinting (3.1 – 5.1). Stationary cycling eliminates wind resistance and removes much of the body weight that must be thrust forward in sprinting. It is theorized that a high speed stationary cycling program for 6-8 weeks that is used as a supplement to other training programs may increase the stride rate of sprinters. To date, there is no research to either support or refute this theory.

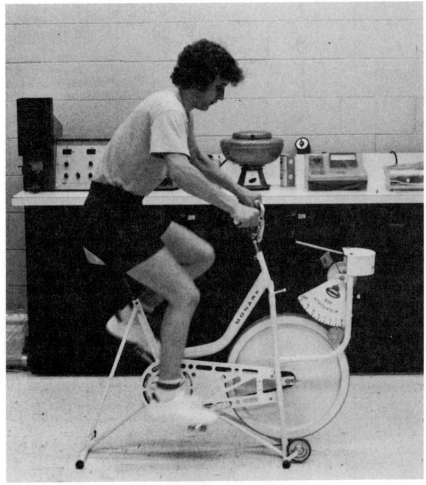

High speed stationary cycling.

Week	Repetitions	Acceleration Distance	Downhill Distance	Repetition Progression	Rest (Min.)
1	2-3	25-35 yds. (4-5 sec.)	15-20yds. (2-3 sec)	Add 1-2 each workout	1-2
2	4-6	25-35 yds.	15-20 yds. (2-3) sec.	Add 1 each workout	2
3	7-9	25-35 yds. (4-5 sec.)	15-20 yds. (2-3 sec.)	Add 1 each workout	3
4	9-10	25-35 yds. (4-5 sec.)	15-20 yds. (2-3 sec.)	Add 1 each workout	3½-4
5	Avoid increasing the number of repetitions beyond 10; merely repeat the workout in week #4. Be certain that you are fully recovered after each repetition.				

Table 7.3 Downhill Sprinting and Cycling Program for Improving Speed in the 40-yard Dash

Treadmill Sprinting

In the Virginia Commonwealth University Laboratory, the A.R. Young high-speed treadmill (0-24.7 mph and sub 8.0 100-yd dash) is used to improve stride length, stride rate, form, anaerobic fitness, and sprinting speed. Cinematography identifies differences in stride length and rate at various speeds in both treadmill and unaided, flat surface sprinting. Form is corrected by an expert standing on a stool facing and looking downward at the subject during high speed sprinting.

The following guidelines were developed in the VCU laboratory:

- Runners use a standard warmup procedure prior to entry on the treadmill.
- A belt attached to the support rails that allows free arm movement, balance, and safety is used. One spotter is placed on each side of the treadbelt.
- A one-week acclimation period is used to allow sprinters to adjust to entry on the treadbelt at high speeds and to treadmill sprinting.
- Since the treadbelt accelerates slowly and would introduce a fatigue factor if sprinters were required to jog at a slow pace and continue running until higher speeds were reached, treadbelt speeds are pre-set prior to entry. After 6-8 practice attempts, entry at high speeds is performed easily.

In using the sample program, keep in mind that sprinters should be in an almost fully recovered state prior to each sprint, since the objective is to improve stride rate and not to improve your conditioning level.

Purpose	Speed	Repetitions
Acclimation	10 percent under maximum	6-20 at 2 min. intervals for 10 seconds.
Entry Practice	25 percent under maximum 10 percent under maximum at maximum speed	10-30 for two seconds
Improved Stride Rate and Length	1-2 mph and 3-4 mph above maximum	2-6 for 3-5 seconds allowing full recovery after each

Table 7.4 Treadmill Sprint Program

Treadmill sprint training is not without its special problems. The treadbelt movement and sprinting action produce a slowing effect; however, aiding factors predominate and allow a faster rate for most individuals even without training. The braking effect has been found to be greater in the initial stages and tends to be eliminated as acclimation occurs and form instruction is given. At high speeds beyond one's maximum speed (in early training sessions) it almost reduces treadbelt speed to a sprinter's maximum speed. This is soon overcome. There are still additional problems. It is difficult to determine true treadbelt speed while a sprinter is performing. There is always a difference between belt speed with and without a sprinter on the treadmill. In one study, a highly accurate surface speed indicator was used to determine belt speed variations with a sprinter (159 lb. and a 197 lb. individual) and without a sprinter. Several findings deserve attention:

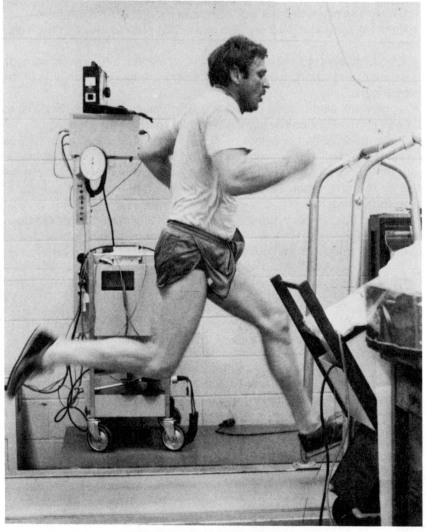

High- speed treadmill sprinting.

	Towing with "Sprint Master"	Stationary Cycling	Treadmill Training	Downhill Training
Effectiveness in Improving 40-yd. Dash Time	Excellent	Unknown?	Excellent	Good
Special Equipment and Cost	Sprint Master: Approx. $600.	Ergometer: $200-400.	High-Speed Treadmill: $5,000 and up	No Cost
Maintenance	Very Little	Oiling	Oiling	None
Safety	Very safe with proper supervision	Very safe even without supervision	Acclimation and very competent spotting, use of a safety belt is needed.	Very safe with proper supervision
Special Needs	Field area with grass or soft terrain	None	None	Slope of approximately 2.6°
Limitations	Probably the best of the four methods; most effective and practical for in-and off-season work in any sport; indoor and outdoor use.	Effectiveness is unknown; not exactly the same movements as sprinting	Cost of treadmill; one-on-one training is slow; inappropriate for groups	Difficult to locate a hill with the proper slope; does not produce as long or fast a stride as towing.

Table 7.5 Comparison of Four Sprint-Assisted Training Programs

- A heavier sprinter has a greater braking affect.
- The percent of braking increases as treadbelt speed increases for both light and heavy subjects.
- At speeds in which the sprinter is being supported by the belt and is unable to maintain belt speed, only a normal expected braking occurs.
- The maximum treadbelt speed without a runner on the A.R. Young Model with Speed Adaptor Kit is 24.77 mph. Maximum speed with a 159 lb. runner was 23.30 mph and with a 197 lb. runner 23.13 mph.

Current research with high-speed treadmill sprinting demonstrates improved stride rate and length with this affect carried over to unaided sprinting.

Sprint-Resisted Training

Sprint-resisted training attempts to simulate the sprinting action while placing the body under an increased work load through use of incline running or weighted clothing. Both programs strive for improved strength in the muscles involved in sprinting. It is impossible to maintain normal stride length or rate while performing under such resistance. Thus, such training is used only in conjunction with regular sprint training on flat surfaces. Uphill running does recruit the fast-twitch (white muscle) motor units and may increase anaerobic fitness. There is little evidence that sprint-resisted training (ankle weights, weighted vests, etc.) improves speed in short distances. It may be more beneficial as an anaerobic conditioning program.

Summary

At least one of the four sprint-assisted training programs should be used two to three times weekly. The most effective and practical program is towing. With the use of the Sprint Master as a towing device, you can take faster and longer strides. Although downhill sprinting is the least expensive method, it does not allow you to take as long or as fast a stride as towing. Treadmill sprinting is also an excellent program; however, the cost of a high speed treadmill capable of reaching speeds of 24-25 mph is prohibitive.

Sprint-assisted training must be performed early in the workout when you are fatigue-free. A fatigued athlete cannot take long strides at super high rates per second.

8

STRENGTH AND POWER TRAINING

A high level of strength and power increases speed by improving stride length, stride rate, starting ability, and acceleration. Take the tests described in Appendix B to evaluate your present level of strength and power in the legs and upper body. Regardless of your strength/power scores, you can benefit from training in this area. This chapter provides a thorough discussion of modern strength/power training designed to improve speed in short distances.

Principles Of Weight Training For Improved Speed

Nine simple principles serve as guidelines in designing your program to increase strength, power, and 40-yard dash time.

Overload

For the development of strength and power, each person has an "optimal load," or an ideal exercise level needed to produce results. Suppose, for example, this optimal load for improving strength in the biceps muscles (front of upper arm) is five repetitions of the curl using 60 pounds on the barbell. Using less than 60 pounds is termed an "under-load" and would not increase strength. Using 70, 80, or 90 pounds represents an "overload" and results in the greatest strength gain.

Your optimal load for strength/power training is approximately 80 per cent of your maximum. Actually, the closer you work to your maximum load for each exercise, the greater the strength gains.

Progressive Resistance Exercise

Muscles must be exercised against a gradually increased resistance. Increased loads beyond the demands regularly made on the body determine the ultimate effectiveness of an exercise program. This principle is applied by increasing the resistance to be overcome, the number of repetitions, the speed of movement, the duration of the training session, decreasing the rest interval and through a combination of each. A training program must, therefore, provide gradual progression in terms of increased load.

Alternate Day Workouts

Strength/power gains occur more rapidly when workouts are scheduled every other day. With one full day of rest between each strength session, muscle groups are fully recovered and have fully benefited from the previous workout. Daily workouts will not improve strength and power as effectively unless an entirely different group of muscles are exercised.

Arrangement or Order of Exercises

Larger muscle groups of the legs and hips should be exercised before the smaller muscles of the arms. Smaller muscles fatigue more quickly and easily than larger muscle groups. To ensure proper overload of the large muscles, they should be exercised before the smaller muscle groups become fatigued. In addition, muscle groups should be alternated to avoid exercising the same group twice in succession. By alternating muscle groups, sufficient recovery time occurs before returning to a previously exercised group. These two concepts (large muscle groups first, alternative muscle groups) are applied by exercising muscle groups in the following order: upper legs and hips, chest and upper arms, back and posterior aspect of legs, lower legs and ankles, shoulders and posterior aspect of upper arms, abdomen, and anterior aspect of upper arms. Sample exercise routines presented in this chapter apply both concepts.

Principle of Specificity

Whenever possible, weight training exercises should simulate the muscular movement for which training is taking place. Strength training to improve speed in short distances must involve exercises similar to actual sprinting movements such as the sprint-arm exercise (arms are rapidly moved back and forth as in the sprinting action), sprinter's kick (same movement as the pushoff from the blocks and the ground surface), and others. The idea is to exercise the exact same muscle groups utilized in sprinting in exactly the same movement pattern. While this is not always possible it can be done in a number of exercises. The specific exercises chosen for speed improvement in this chapter attempt to apply this principle.

Positive and Negative Work

There are two distinct phases of a weight training exercise. The weight is raised (positive phase) and, after a brief pause, it is lowered (negative phase). The muscle contracts and shortens during the positive phase and relaxes and stretches during the negative phase. For each repetition, the same muscles are used for both the positive and negative phases of the exercise and each phase contributes to strength/power development. Weight should be raised explosively and lowered slowly for speed improvement. Arching the back, jerking the weight, or cheating in any manner to secure better leverage merely lessens the benefits and increases the possibility of injury.

Although momentary muscular fatigue is reached quicker during the positive phase, muscles can lower more weight (negative) than they can raise. If the negative phase is done correctly, the workout will be much more productive. Research indicates that lowering the resistance is far more important for strength development than raising the resistance. If you take one second to raise the weight, it should take two seconds, or twice as long, to lower the weight.

Maintenance

One weight training workout weekly, preferably the last item on your Wednesday schedule, will maintain most of the strength and power gains you acquired in the off-season. Three sets of 5 repetitions (using the 5 RM) should be used for each exercise.

Proper Breathing

Breath should not be held during muscular contraction. The recommended breathing procedure is to inhale as the weight is lowered and to exhale as the weight is raised or pushed away from the body. You should attempt to blow the weight away from the body. This procedure will improve your efficiency and reduce the risk of "blacking out" during a demanding exertion. Until the correct technique is mastered, correct inhaling and exhaling should be practiced using light weights.

Warm-up and Warm-down

To avoid possible injury to muscles and joints, a 10-15 minute warmup period of stretching and calisthenic movements is suggested (see Chapter 6). The use of light-to-moderate weight for the first set of each exercise will also help reduce the risk of injury from muscle strain.

At the close of the strength training session, it is helpful to perform 3-5 minutes of stretching for the back and front of the upper legs and the trunk. A short version of the warmup routine described in Chapter 6 can be used to stretch the major muscle groups that have been exposed to heavy weights.

Training Variables

A number of training variables must also be manipulated correctly to guarantee strength/power and speed improvement. It is critical that these factors be carefully controlled if improved speed is to occur.

Repetitions

The number of times an exercise is performed without any intervening rest period gradually increases from the lower limit to the upper limit every 3-5 workouts. For speed improvement, repetitions should be low (1-5).

Sets

The number of times a group of repetitions is performed each workout is referred to a set. All exercises should be completed once before repeated sets are used. One to three sets are recommended.

Rest Interval

The amount of rest between each exercise should be minimal. Sample programs in Tables 8.2 and 8.3 alternate muscle groups after each exercise and permit you to move from one to another with no rest. Time pressures in team sports are such that an entire workout must be completed in fifteen minutes or less. By eliminating the rest interval and "socializing" after each exercise, this is sufficient time for an effective workout.

Weight (RM = Repetitions Maximum)

The weight that permits you to perform a specific number of repetitions is termed the RM. The 3 RM, then, is the amount of weight with which you can perform only three repetitions. When working with 1-5 repetitions, the 3 RM is chosen as a starting weight. As soon as you can complete 5 repetitions of an exercise, additional weight is added (5-10 lbs. for upper body and 10-20 lbs. for lower body exercises) and you return to one repetition on the next workout.

Speed of Contraction

If speed is the desired outcome, rapid, explosive movements should be used on each exercise. Weight should be lowered (negative) slowly, however, after the explosive lift.

Lifting Techniques

The following techniques apply to practically any weight training exercise:
- For the basic stance, place the feet slightly wider than shoulder width with the toes parallel. Primary considerations are balance (maintaining the weight directly above the medial plane of the body) and agility. The stronger leg is sometimes placed back in a heel-toe alignment (left heel is even with the right toe), depending upon your preference.
- Toes should be placed just under the bar in the starting phase of exercises where the barbell is resting on the floor.
- Maintain an erect back (unless this is the muscle group being exercised) with head up and eyes looking straight ahead.
- Refrain from altering the stabilizing body parts after the exercise is initiated.
- Stress mechanical disadvantages of levers in arm exercises.
- Practice adequate safety precautions at all times and use a partner to spot on exercises involving heavy weight:
  - Avoid attempting to move more weight than you can safely handle.
  - Secure collars and engage pins before attempting any type of lift.
  - Stay clear of an individual engaging in a lift.
  - Avoid distractions while another person is concentrating on a lift.

—Avoid holding your breath while lifting heavy weights.
—Practice returning all weights to the floor or rack in a controlled manner
—Bend the knees when attempting to move heavy weights from one place to another for storage.
—Protect the back by developing strong abdominal muscles.

• Grasp the bar at approximately shoulder width with the weight equally distributed on each hand. Utilize the alternate grip when heavy weights must be supported by the arms, as in the dead and straddle lifts:

Grips

Alternate Grip: The alternate grip is a combination of the pronated and supinated styles, with one hand assuming a pronated and the other a supinated grip in order to reduce finger strain in heavy lifts.

Pronated Grip: In the pronated or overhand grip, the bar is grasped until the thumb wraps around and meets the index finger. The thumb may be placed next to the index finger without wrapping around the bar if so desired in a particular lift.

Supinated Grip: In the supinated or underhand grip, the bar is grasped with the palms turned upward away from the body. The fingers and thumb are wrapped around as indicated above.

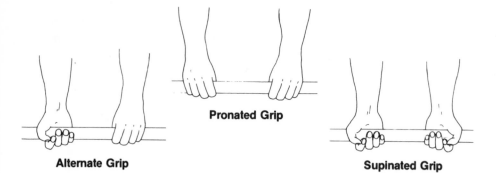

Pronated Grip

Alternate Grip

Supinated Grip

Exercises

Strength/power exercises are chosen on the basis of the involvement with the muscles affecting the sprinting action (see Table 8.1). Each exercise must be performed with rapid, explosive contractions using heavy weights (3 RM), multiple sets (1-5), low repetitions (3-5), and include power-type exercises.

Table 8.1. Basic Exercises for Speed Improvement

Exercise	Equipment	Basic Movement	Helpful Hints	Muscle Groups Activated
Upper body 1. Bench press.	Barbell, bench rack.	Pronated grip, lying on the back on a bench or floor, with both knees raised, the bar is slowly lowered to the chest and pressed back to the starting position.	Keep both feet flat on the floor; avoid lifting the buttocks; extend the arms fully.	Shoulder extensors.
2. Bent-arm pullover.	Barbell, bench rack.	Pronated grip; from the same position as above the bar is placed at the chest and lowered behind the end of a bench (arms flexed) as far as possible before a return arch brings the bar back to the starting position.	Flex the arms during the entire movement; pass the bar close to the face on the return phase.	Shoulder flexors. Arm and shoulder extensors.
3. Curl.	Barbell.	Supinated grip; with the bar resting at the thighs and the arms fully extended, the bar is raised to chest level and returned.	Keep all parts of the body erect and motionless throughout; use less weight than in the two-arm curl.	Upper arm flexors, wrist flexors, long finger flexors.
4. Forward raise.	Barbell.	Pronated grip; from a standing position, with the bar resting at the thighs, the arms move upward to the height of the shoulders and return in the same arch.	Keep the entire body erect at all times, vary the exercise by continuing the movement to the overhead position.	Flexors, anterior and middle deltoid.
5. Lateral raise.	Dumbbells.	Pronated grip; both arms are extended from the thighs outward to head level and lowered to the starting position.	Maintain an erect upper-lower torso; avoid flexing arms; vary with the leaning raise (same movement with trunk flexed at right angles) or supine position (lying on back on floor or bench).	Abductors, shoulder horizontal flexors.
6. Military press.	Barbell.	Pronated grip; the bar is slowly pushed overhead from chest level until both arms are fully extended.	Maintain an erect neck and back, and extended, locked knees; avoid jerky movements or lean.	Abductors, flexors, and arm extensors.

Exercise	Equipment	Technique	Key Points	Muscles
7. Rowing.	Barbell.	Pronated grip; with the bar resting at the thighs and the arms and legs extended, the bar is raised to the chin and returned to the thigh rest position.	Use a narrow grip with the hands 6-8 inches apart; keep the elbows higher than the hands; maintain an erect stationary position.	Abductors, arm flexors.
8. Shoulder shrug.	Barbell.	Pronated grip; with the bar resting at the thigh and the body erect, both shoulders are elevated until they nearly contact the face before relaxing and permitting the bar to return to the starting position.	Keep the extremities fully extended; heavy weight will insure more rapid strength gains.	Shoulder girdle elevators
9. Sprint arm exercise.	Dumbbells.	Pronated grip; with one foot slightly ahead, knees flexed, body forward, work arms to simulate the sprinting action.	Dumbbells should move between the shoulder and hip.	Anterior and posterior thoracic muscles and upper arm muscles.
10. Straight-arm pullover.	Barbell.	Pronated grip; lying on a bench, with the head at the very edge, the barbell resting on the floor, and both arms extended, the bar is raised overhead and returned to the floor.	Maintain fully extended arms; do not elevate the lower back or remove the feet from the floor.	Pectoralis muscles, triceps, latissimus dorsi, serratus anterior.
11. Two-handed snatch.	Power rack.	Pronated grip; bar is raised in one continuous motion from the floor to an extended position overhead and held for 2 seconds.	Place hands slightly wider than shoulder width, keep body directly under the weight at all times.	Abductors, flexors, arm extensors, lower leg and back extensors, quadriceps, hamstrings, gluteus maximus.
12. Two-handed clean and jerk.	Power rack.	Pronated grip; bar is brought in one continuous motion up to the chest through use of the squat or split. Bar must be raised overhead with elbows and knees locked for 2 seconds.	The bar may not contact the chest, perform movement as rapidly as possible.	Abductors, flexors, quadriceps, gastrocnemius, foot plantar flexors, lower leg and back extensors.

Abdominal

Exercise	Equipment	Description	Technique	Muscles
13. Side bender.	Barbell.	Pronated grip; with the bar in the shoulder rest position, the upper torso is alternately tilted to the right and left and brought back to the starting position.	Tilt as far as possible to each side; secure bar collars; perform movement with dumbbell in each hand.	Lateral flexors.
14. Situps (bent leg).	Barbell or disc.	Pronated grip; from a supine position on the back, with the bar or weight held firmly behind the neck with both hands, the upper torso is raised until both elbows contact the knees.	Bring heels up tight with the buttocks; flex the neck forward to initiate the movement; hook feet under a bar.	Hip flexors, psoas major.
15. Situps (straight leg).	Barbell or disc.	Pronated grip; from the position described in No. 14 the upper torso is raised until both elbows contact the knees.	Same as for No. 14; vary by alternately touching opposite elbow to opposite knee.	Rectus abdominus.

Back

Exercise	Equipment	Description	Technique	Muscles
16. Dead lift (straight leg).	Barbell.	Alternate grip; with the bar at the thigh rest position, the hips are flexed to lower the bar without flexing the legs.	Maintain arms and legs fully extended; use light weights.	Back and hip extensors.
17. Dead lift (overhead straight leg).	Barbell.	Pronated grip; from a standing position, the upper torso lowers to grasp the bar, with the arms fully extended, before raising the weight in a semicircle to a position overhead.	Extend legs and arms; avoid jerky movements; use light weight.	Back and leg extensors, arm flexors.
18. Dead lift (flexed knees).	Barbell.	Alternate grip; with the bar resting on the floor, a crouch position is assumed, the knees are flexed, the arms and back extended; the bar is raised to the thigh rest position and lowered.	Maintain extended arms and erect back; lift weight by extending the knees and hips and moving to a standing position; keep the shoulders back to protect the back muscles.	Thigh, lower leg, and back extensors; quadriceps; hamstrings, gluteus maximus.

Exercise	Equipment	Technique	Notes	Muscles
19. Trunk flexor.	Barbell.	Pronated grip; from a standing position, with the bar in the shoulder rest position, the upper body is bent forward to a right angle, parallel to the floor, and then returned to the upright position.	Keep the head up; avoid bending the knees; alter the movement with hyper-extension of the trunk and/or twisting to the right or left as the body is returned to the starting position.	Back extensors.
20. Balance shoot.	Iron boots.	Sitting position, raise legs simultaneously before drawing to chest, straighten and repeat.	Keep legs off floor until a set is completed.	Quadriceps, iliopsoas, rectus abdominas obliques.
21. Bench knee extension.	Bench and lower bar.	Hook ankles in bar and bend backwards before returning to a sitting position.	Alter angle of body to increase tension.	Supporting muscles of the knee.

Lower Torso

Exercise	Equipment	Technique	Notes	Muscles
22. Heel raise.	Barbell, 2 to 3 inch board.	Pronated grip; with the bar in the shoulder rest position, the toes together elevated on a 2-3 inch board, the body is raised upward to the maximum height of the toes.	Alter toe position from straight ahead, to pointed in and out; keep the body erect.	Foot plantar flexors.
23. Hip flexor.	Iron boots.	From a standing position, the knees are alternately pulled toward the abdominal area and returned.	Perform this movement with explosiveness; combine with alternate knee extensor.	Hip flexors.
24. Knee curl.	Iron boots.	Lying on back, raise legs simultaneously upward then draw rapidly to chest before extending legs and returning to starting position.	Rapid movement is stressed.	Quadriceps, iliopsoas.
25. Knee extensor.	Iron boots, bench or table.	From a sitting position, with the lower legs extended over a table, the foot is raised by extending the knees alternately.	Maintain an erect back; stabilize the body by grasping the sides of the table.	Quadriceps group.
26. Knee flexor.	Iron boots.	From a standing position, the knees are alternately flexed to move the boot as close to the buttocks as possible.	Can also be performed lying flat on the stomach; keep the body erect.	Hamstrings.

Exercise	Equipment	Description	Notes	Muscle group
27. Leg abductor.	Iron boots.	Lying on one side with the boot secured to the top, the weight is raised upward as far as possible and returned to the starting position.	Stabilize the body by resting the head on a bent arm, maintaining floor contact with the other hand.	Abductors.
28. Medial ligament abductor.	Wall pulley.	With strap around ankle, knee flexed, hip abducted, the leg is pulled inward and forward.	Use when softening of a cartilage is present.	Supporting muscles of the knee.
29. Modified leg lift.	Iron boots.	From a sitting position with the back erect and hands grasping a chair, the legs are lifted from the floor.	Keep back erect at all times.	Quadriceps.
30. Modified hip flexor.	Vaulting horse, iron boots.	Lying prone along the horse with one pommel removed and height adjusted to allow feet to rest comfortably on the floor, the upper leg is flexed and brought toward the abdominal area.	Perform repetitions with one leg, then the other, begin with only the boot.	Hip flexors.
31. One-legged squat.	Dumbbells.	Pronated grip; from a standing position with a dumbbell in both hands, squat rapidly to right angles and return to upright position.	Toe in slightly with the base foot, begin without use of dumbbells, avoid using back muscles to straighten, remain on the toes.	Thigh and lower leg extensors.
32. Quadriceps exercise.	Iron boot.	Lying on back with one leg in iron boot elevated at 90° against a wall, leg is elevated to right angles and returned.	Quadriceps exercise for chondromalacia of the patella.	Quadriceps.
33. Rhythm lift.	Barbell, padded shoulder rest support.	Pronated grip; with the bar in the shoulder rest position, back erect, knees slightly flexed, bounce on balls of feet trying to reach maximum height on each bounce. One repetition or bounce per second for 60 seconds.	Keep feet at shoulder width, bounce only on balls of feet, do not return to surface on heels or with knees locked.	Foot plantar flexors, gastrocnemius.

Exercise	Equipment	Description	Notes	Muscles
34. Squat.	Barbell, squat rack, bench, 2-3 inch board.	Pronated grip; with the bar in the shoulder rest position, the body is lowered to a sitting position by flexing the legs until the buttocks contact the chair or bench placed underneath the body.	Avoid bending the back; keep the head up; point the toes outward slightly with heels elevated on 2-3 inch board.	Thigh and lower leg extensors.
35. Squat jump.	Dumbbells.	Pronated grip; with the feet in a heel-toe alignment and the body in a squat position (dumbbell in each hand), a forceful jump, or extension is performed that completely extends and raises both legs from the floor. Foot position is reversed in mid-air before the body is returned to the starting position.	Maintain an erect position throughout; strive for maximum height on each jump; work from the balls of the feet.	Lower leg, thigh, and back extensors.
36. Squat walk.	Barbell, padded shoulder rest support.	Pronated grip; with the bar in the shoulder rest position, short steps (1-2 feet) are taken while squatting down toward the real heel after each step until the thigh of the front leg is parallel to the floor.	After each step and squat raise the body to a normal walking position; number of steps fulfill the repetition variable.	Thigh and lower leg extensors.
37. Straddle lift.	Barbell.	Alternate grip; from a standing position, the upper torso is lowered to grasp the bar, with the arms fully extended and the body is returned to the starting position. One leg is placed on each side of the bar at shoulder width apart.	Grasp the bar with one arm toward both ends; keep head, back, and shoulders erect.	Thigh, lower leg, and back extensors.
38. Supine leg lift.	Iron boots.	Lying on the back, the legs are alternately raised, with the knees straight, to a vertical position.	Keep the lower back in constant contact with the floor; grasp a weighted barbell overhead to stabilize the upper torso.	Quadriceps.

Table 8.2. Off-Season Program for Speed Improvement

Exercises	Repetitions	Sets	Starting Weight	Speed of Contraction	Interval* Minutes to Seconds
Basic Program:					
Bench press	3-5	3	3 RM	Rapid	2 to 30
Squat (¾, ½)/ leg press	3-5	3	3 RM	Rapid	2 to 30
Rhythm lift	Maximum	2	Squat weight	Rapid	2 to 30
		3	3 RM	Rapid	2 to 30
Upright rowing	6-9	2	6 RM	Rapid	2 to 30
Sprintarm exercise	6-9	3	5 lbs.	Rapid	2 to 30
Sprinter's kick	6-9	3	3 RM	Rapid	2 to 30
Knee flexor	3-5	3	3 RM	Rapid	2 to 30
Knee extensor	3-5	3	6 RM	Rapid	2 to 30
Hamstring stretching	15-25	2	Body only	Slow, static	0 to 30
Alternate I: Lower Torso Concentration					
Military Press	3-5	3	6 RM	Rapid	2 to 30
Squat	3-5	3	6 RM	Rapid	2 to 30
Heel raise	6-9	3	6 RM	Rapid	2 to 30
Straddle lift	3-5	3	3 RM	Rapid	2 to 30
Hip flexor	3-5	3	3 RM	Rapid	2 to 30
Supine leg lift	3-5	3	3 RM	Rapid	2 to 30
Leg abductor	3-5	3	3 RM	Rapid	2 to 30
Hamstring stretching	15-25	2	Body only	Slow, static	0 to 30
Alternate II: Lower Torso Concentration					
Pullover : (straight)	6-9	3	6 RM	Rapid	2 to 30
Squat jump	6-9	3	6 RM	Rapid	2 to 30
Military press	3-5	3	3 RM	Rapid	2 to 30
Knee flexor	3-5	3	3 RM	Rapid	2 to 30
Knee extensor	3-5	3	3 RM	Rapid	2 to 30
Straight-arm pullover	3-5	3	3 RM	Rapid	2 to 30
Leg abductor	3-5	3	3 RM	Rapid	2 to 30
Hamstring stretching	15-25	2	Body only	Slow, static	0 to 30

Upper Body Exercises for the Improvement of Sprinting

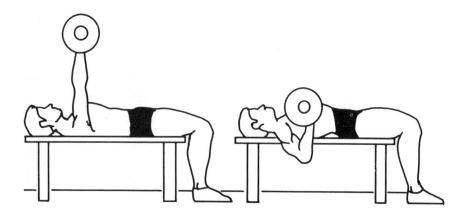

Bench Press

Military Press

Rowing

Curl

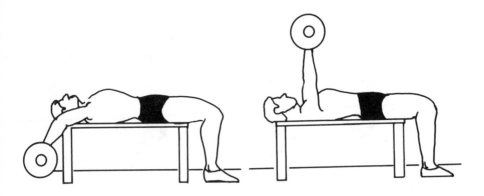

Straight-arm Pull-over

Lower Torso Exercises for the Improvement of Sprinting Speed

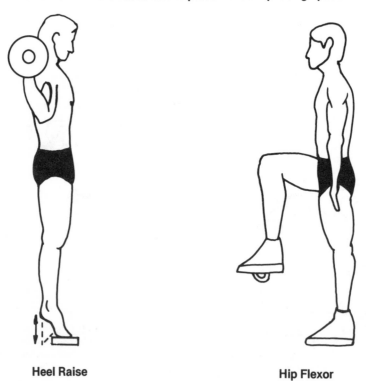

Heel Raise

Hip Flexor

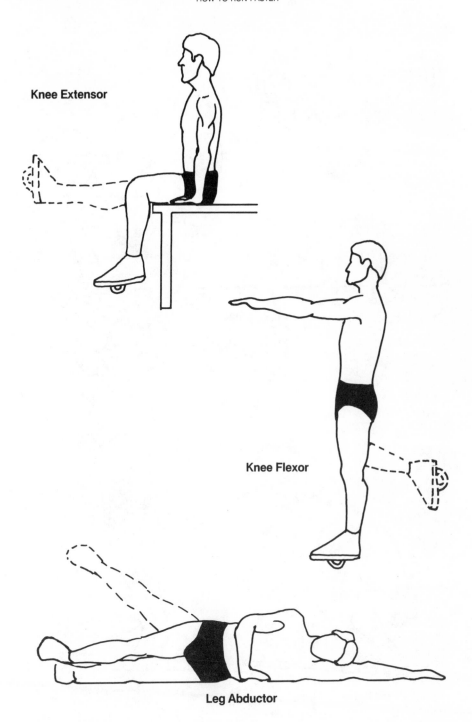

Knee Extensor

Knee Flexor

Leg Abductor

Squat

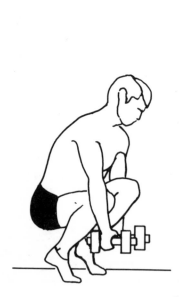
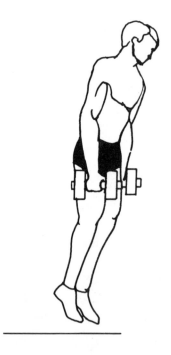

Squat Jump

Straddle Lift

Supine Leg Lift

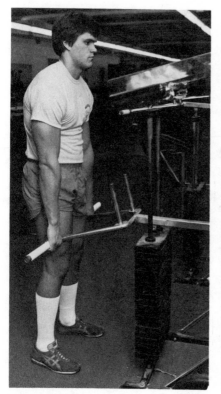 

Shoulder Shrug

Dead Lift
(straight leg)

Lateral Raise (standing position)

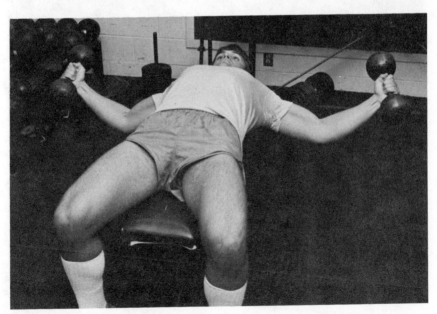

Lateral Raise (supine position)

Situps

Table 8.3. In-season Program for Speed Improvement

Exercises	Repetitions	Sets	Starting Weight	Speed of Contraction	Interval Minutes to Seconds
Bench press	3-5	3	3 RM	Rapid	2 to 30
Squat (3/4, 1/2) (leg press)	3-5	3	3 RM	Rapid	2 to 30
Rhythm lift	Maximum	2	Squat Weight	Rapid	2 to 30
Sprinter's kick	6-9	3	3 RM	Rapid	2 to 30
Sprint arm exercise	6-9	3	6 RM	Rapid	2 to 30
Hamstring stretching	15-25	2	—	Slow	30

Basic Strength/Power Training For Speed Improvement

The basic steps in the development of a strength/power training program for speed improvement are to identify the muscles involved in the sprinting action and choose exercises that activate these muscles to alter variables in a manner conducive to speed improvement. Use the basic program for 1-2 months, changing to alternate programs periodically after this period, and use the basic exercises shown in Table 8.3 during the in-season period twice weekly (once weekly following the Wednesday practice session if seeking only to maintain the strength/power gains acquired previously).

Special Strength/Power Training Methods For Speed Improvement

A number of special programs can be used for variation or for specific exercises to improve strength, power, and speed. These approaches are extremely demanding, involve handling very heavy weights and require working out with a partner who assists and protects you during each exercise.

The Groves Super Overload Method

Barney Groves, Ph.D., has developed a method with the potential for superior strength/power gains for sprinters which is highly applicable to the bench press, leg press and ankle exercises. Follow these steps:

- Establish your 1RM.
- Add 25 per cent more weight to this amount.
- Begin the first repetition of each exercise in the "up" position (Bench Press—exercise begins with arms extended overhead, elbows locked; leg press—partner helps you to extend your legs and lock both knees).
- The first repetition is only a slight 2-3" bend of the joint.
- Continue taking the weight downward, further each time, until on the 7th repetition, you are unable to return the weight to the up position.
- Complete 3 sets of 7 repetitions every other day; at the end of each week, redetermine your 1RM and repeat these steps using the new weight.

The Superload Method allows you to work with much heavier weight than traditional programs. Greater strength/power gains occur in areas that are critical to sprinting: upper arms and shoulders, upper and lower legs, and ankles. Specific exercises that should be performed using this method are indicated in Table 8.1.

Rest-Pause Method

A single repetition is performed at near maximum weight (1RM) before resting 1-2 minutes, completing a second repetition, resting again, and so on until the muscle is fatigued and cannot perform even one repetition.

Set System

The use of multiple sets is one of the most popular advanced training methods. Several repetitions of an exercise are performed before repeating the exercise, resting, and repeating it again. Three to four sets of approximately 5-6 repetitions are used for each exercise.

Burnout

For each exercise, 75 per cent of the maximal weight is used to complete as many consecutive repetitions as possible. After a one-minute rest, ten pounds are removed from the starting weight and another set is completed. After another one minute rest period, ten more pounds are removed and a third set is completed, and so on, until the muscle group is totally fatigued.

Wipeout

For each exercise, 50 per cent of the maximum weight is used to complete as many consecutive repetitions as possible. When you can no longer perform another repetition, a one-minute rest period is taken before completing a second and third set with the same starting weight. This procedure is continued with a rest period of not more than one minute until you have completely exhausted the muscle group.

Supersets

A set of exercises for one group of muscles is followed immediately by a set for their antagonist. A variation of this method is known as "super multiple sets" and consists of performing three sets of an exercise for one group of muscles followed by the same number of sets for their antagonists. A short rest is taken between sets. For example, one set of arm curls (biceps muscle — agonist) is followed by a set of bench presses (triceps — antagonist).

A superset consists of performing three sets of an exercise for one group of muscles followed by the same number of sets for their antagonists.

Special Equipment

Universal Gym

The Universal Gym provides variable resistance and can be used to perform many of the barbell exercises described in Table 8.1. Stacked weights travel up and down on fixed tracks and make weight change adjustments convenient by simply removing and inserting a metal pin at each station. This arrangement eliminates many of the safety hazards so prevalent with free weights. The Universal Gym is a versatile piece of equipment; it is easy to operate and can be repositioned by one person. The main disadvantage of the Universal Gym is its inability to simulate some of the key exercises that are important to speed improvement.

Universal Gym exercises for speed improvement

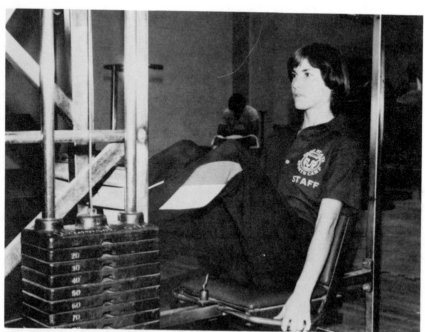

Leg Press

Seated Press

Biceps Curl

Heel Raise

Lat Pulldown

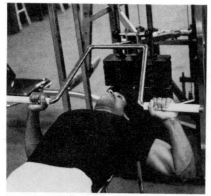

Bench Press

Triceps Extension

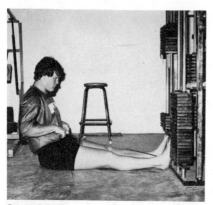

Seated Row

Leg Curl

Situp

Leg Extension

Nautilus

Nautilus equipment is designed to work a single muscle group through a full range of motion. The name, "Nautilus" comes from the resistance pulley which is shaped like a nautilus shell. The counterweight is "timed" like an automobile ignition system in order to provide the same resistance throughout the full range of movement. Strict emphasis is placed on proper form for one set of each exercise. Some disadvantages of the Nautilus system are the cost, the need for 8-15 different machines to accomplish a complete workout, the large space needed to house the equipment, and the fact that the machines do not duplicate many of the key exercises that are important to speed improvement.

Nautilus exercises for speed improvement

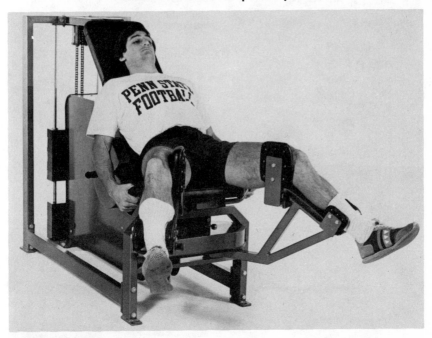

Adductor Exercise

Seated Press

Pullover

Side Bender

Double Chest

Double Shoulder

Leg Curl

Leg Extension

Hip and Back

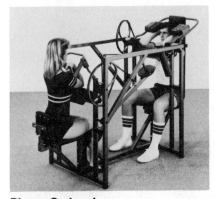

**Biceps Curl and
Triceps Extension**

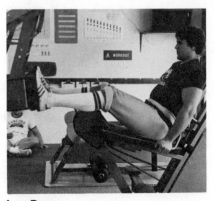

Leg Press

A basic Nautilus and Universal Gym program for speed improvement is shown in Table 8.4.

Exercises	Repetitions	Sets	Starting Weight	Speed of* Contraction	Interval Minutes to Seconds**
Universal Gym:					
Knee flexion	3-5	3	3 RM	Rapid	2 to 30
Bench press	3-5	3	3 RM	Rapid	2 to 30
Leg press	3-5	3	3 RM	Rapid	2 to 30
Rhythm lift	Maximum	3	Leg press Weight	Rapid	2 to 30
Sprinter's kick	6-9	3	6 RM	Rapid	2 to 30
Knee extension	3-5	3	3 RM	Rapid	2 to 30
Curl	3-5	3	3 RM	Slow	2 to 30
Hamstring stretching	15-25	2	—	Slow	30 seconds
Nautilus:					
Hip & back	6-9	2	6 RM	Rapid	2 to 30
Leg extension	6-9	2	6 RM	Rapid	2 to 30
Leg press	6-9	2	6 RM	Rapid	2 to 30
Leg curl	6-9	2	6 RM	Rapid	2 to 30
Bench press	6-9	2	6 RM	Rapid	2 to 30
Curl	6-9	1	6 RM	Slow	2 to 30
Heel raise	Maximum	2	Leg press Weight	Rapid	2 to 30
Hamstring stretching	15-25	2	—	Slow	30 seconds

* The positive phase of each exercise should be done rapidly, followed by a slow return of the weight to the starting position (negative phase).
** The rest interval between each exercise and set should be gradually reduced over a two-month period from two minutes to 30 seconds.

Table 8.4. Nautilius and Universal Gym Program for Speed Improvement

Summary

Strength/power training is essential to speed improvement. Additional strength and power will increase stride length by increasing the force of the pushoff with each step, improve acceleration through the use of more efficient power, and improve stride rate through more powerful contractions of large motor units. Free weights form the foundation of the program. Although not as effective in exercising the exact motor units involved in sprinting, Universal Gym and Nautilus may be used. Strength training should take place every other day as the very last item on the workout.

9
PLYOMETRICS

The word plyometric is derived from the Greek word *plethyein*, meaning to increase, and the word isometric. Basically, it is a hopping and jumping routine used by athletes in Germany, USSR, and recently in the United States to bridge the gap between strength and power (rate of work = force X velocity).There is evidence that the 1972 Olympic 100- and 200-meter winner from the USSR, Valery Borzov, used plyometric drills on a regular basis in his training program. Experts attribute the unexpected victory of Borzov partially to plyometric training. The East Germans and Russians have been using plyometric training for sprinters for a number of years.

Plyometrics are an excellent method of developing both strength and power in the muscles involved in sprinting. Research suggests that speed in short sprints is improved when plyometrics are used in conjunction with other speed improvement programs described in this book. Many athletes have superior strength, yet cannot produce the necessary power to sprint a fast 40-yard dash. Plyometric training is designed to bridge this gap between strength and power as well as to improve the explosive action of jumping from one foot to the other which we call sprinting.

*This chapter was written by Plyometrics expert John Dolan, Football Coach, Randolph Macon College, Ashland, Virginia.

How Plyometrics Work

The best way to obtain maximum power from a muscle group is to pre-stretch the muscles (lengthen) before an explosive muscle contraction occurs (shortening). In other words, you can generate more power in any muscle group by first starting a movement in the opposite direction. The golf and tennis swing and hitting in baseball are examples of pre-stretching by movement in the opposite direction before the explosive swing occurs. Plyometrics do exactly the same thing by first moving the legs in the opposite direction smoothly (flexion) before braking (stopping the movement) and exploding into a hop or jump. This procedure of producing a stronger explosive movement (concentric contraction) when it follows pre-stretching (movement in the opposite direction-eccentric contraction) exploits what is known as the *stretch or myostatic reflex*. Muscles resist stretching by stimulating the stretch receptors or muscle spindles, resulting in proprioceptive nerve impulses traveling to the spinal cord and returning to the same muscle. As a result, a powerful contraction occurs to prevent overstretching. It is possible to exert as much as two times more tension during the explosive phase (eccentric contraction) if the muscle group has first been pre-stretched through a concentric contraction. The explosive movement (jump or hop) must immediately and smoothly follow the pre-stretching phase or movement in the opposite direction.

The use of the pre-stretch principle with plyometrics develops additional strength and power in the key muscle groups for sprinters.

Plyometrics For Speed Improvement

The following guidelines were used to design a plyometric training program for the improvement of speed in short distances:
• The rate at which a muscle is stretched is more important than the distance it is stretched.
• The faster a muscle is forced to lengthen, the greater the tension it exerts.
• The closer the stretch of the muscle is to the contraction, the more violent the contraction.
• In order to assure strength/power gains, the overload principle must be applied; work must be performed with a greater load and intensity than the legs are normally accustomed to doing.
• Short distance hopping of 15-30 yards should be used the first few weeks to acclimate athletes to plyometrics; in subsequent weeks longer distances of up to 100 yards can be used.

- When jumping from boxes or bleachers, the legs should not "give" before rebounding into the next jump.
- Heel cups should be used and drills should be done on soft surfaces such as grass or mats to protect the feet.

Specific Plyometric Drills

Four basic types of hopping and jumping routines can be used in a Plyometric workout to improve speed: *power hops, distance hops, speed hops,* and *depth jumping.* A number of variations exist within each category to help maintain interest. Keep in mind that this type of training is extremely tiring and should be used only by highly conditioned athletes as the final aspect of a workout. To determine whether you should use Plyometrics, take the leg strenth test described in Appendix B on the Universal Gym or Nautilus leg station. Avoid plyometric training until you can leg press 2½ times your body weight. Plyometrics should be used twice weekly on days when you are not training with weights.

Power Plyometrics

Power Hops (double-leg and single-leg takeoff). Athletes form a line at the end of a row of matting, jump as high as possible with no concern for forward speed, and emphasize the knee bend (to pre-stretch), an upward leap with no hesitation or stutter step, and full extension while in the air. Each jump is a maximum effort upward covering about 2-3 feet with the trunk erect and the knees bent to slightly below a 90° angle. Emphasis is placed on height and "hang time" rather than speed. Power plyometrics are the most fatiguing of any type and caution is needed to prevent over exertion.

Power Hops (single leg)

Begin your power hops with 40 yards and increase that distance by 10 yards each week until 70-100 yards is reached.

Power Hops (double-leg)

Power Hurdling (two-foot takeoff)

Power Hurdling (two-foot takeoff). Athletes jump over 5-10 low hurdles placed approximately 6′ apart. Begin with two hurdles, adding one hurdle each week until ten hurdles can be jumped.

**Stationary Power Jumping
(single-leg takeoff)**

**Stationary Power Jumping
(double-leg takeoff)**

Stationary Power Jumping (double-leg and single-leg takeoff). Maximum power upward jumps for 30-60 seconds are executed with the takeoff and landing occuring in the same spot. The arms should be thrust vigorously upward with each jump. When the feet hit the floor, you should immediately jump again as high as possible without a stutter step between leaps. A mark on the wall can be used to determine whether you are using maximum power on each jump (touch that mark each time).

Distance Plyometrics

Distance Hops (double-leg and single-leg takeoff). Athletes hop (each jump as far as possible) for the length of the gymnasium with as few jumps as possible. Competition between athletes can be created by counting the number of bounds it takes to cover a given distance with a double, or single, leg takeoff.

Distance Hops (double-leg takeoff)

Distance Hops (single-leg takeoff)

Speed Plyometrics

Speed Hops (double-leg takeoff). You should hop with both legs before attempting single leg hops to lessen the possibility of a muscle injury. When executing the double-leg speed hop, hop as fast as possible in a series of jumps for 30–75 yards.

Speed Hops (single-leg takeoff). The same procedure as described for the double-leg takeoff is used; however, a 15-20 yard sprint precedes the 30-75 yard single leg hopping at high speed. You should alternate left and right legs each repetition. This movement is recommended as part of your diagnosis in the initial testing session (40-yard one-legged hop) described in Chapter 2.

Speed Hops (double-leg takeoff)

Speed Hops (single-leg takeoff)

Bench Jumping (double-leg takeoff)

Speed Bench Jumping (double-and single-leg takeoff). Athletes stand on one side of a bench and explosively jump to the other side, then back again, continuing this rapid jumping with no stutter step for 15-45 seconds.

Stationary Speed Jumping (double-leg takeoff). Maximum speed upward jumps are performed for 30-60 seconds. The takeoffs and landings occur in the same spot.

Speed Jump-Tucks (double-leg takeoff). Athletes jump as high and as fast as possible, bringing the knees to the chest while in the air. Jumps are performed as rapidly and explosively as possible in a 15-30 second interval.

**Stationary Jumping
(double-leg takeoff)**

Depth Jumps. Athletes jump upward as forcefully as possible with both legs after a straight-line drop is made from a height of 2½- 3 feet. A fast, active takeoff after landing is stressed. In a gymnasium, you can drop nearly straight down onto a mat from the first row of bleachers or from a chair.

In order to obtain the proper platform height, the coach should begin with a height of 12 inches. The platform height is then gradually increased until you can no longer jump up to the starting position.

Box Jumping (double-leg takeoff). Athletes jump up onto and down from a series of boxes, emphasizing a straight-line drop and maximum height on each jump. Russian researchers recommend 18″, 30″ and 40″ boxes.

A

B

C

Box Jumping (3 photo sequence)

Staircase Hopping (two-foot takeoff). Athletes hop up a series of steps before turning and repeating the procedure down the stairs. Proper supervision is needed at all times to prevent injury.

Maximum Effort Jumps

The most effective maximum effort routine using plyometrics is to sprint for 15-25 yards before going into high speed single leg hops until you are completely exhausted and unable to continue. A second repetition is performed using the opposite leg. The drill ends with high speed double leg hops to exhaustion. For variation, any of the previously mentioned hopping and jumping routines can be used. A contest can be held to see which athlete covers the greatest distance, jumps over a bench the most times, or is the last jumper to remain standing. This drill is designed for use with only the most highly conditioned athletes and is used as the final aspect of the workout (see Maximum Effort Training, Chapter 10).

Maximum Effort Jumps

Type	Distance	Repetitions	Rest Interval	Progression
Power Hops	30 yards	2 (double leg) 2 (left leg) 2 (right leg)	1½ min.	Add 5 yards weekly to a maximum of 75 yards
Distance Hops	30 yards	Same as above	1 min.	Same as above
Speed Hops	30 yards	Same as above	1 min.	Add 10 yards weekly to a maximum of 100 yards
Depth Jumps	30 yards	Same as above	1 min.	Add 5 yards weekly to a maximum of 75 yards.
Maximum Effort Hops	Maximum	1 (double leg) 1 (left leg) 1 (right leg)	1 min.	Record the distance covered each week to determine gains

Warmup: light running-in-place, lifting knees to waist level for 2-4 minutes, followed by easy jumping and hopping (double and single leg take-off) for two lengths of the gymasium.

Variations: Variations of different jumps and hops should be used weekly to maintain interest.

Table 9.1. Plyometric Workout and Progression

Summary

Plyometric training is designed to bridge the gap between strength and power. It has been shown to improve sprinting speed when used in conjunction with other training programs. A series of hopping and jumping exercises are used that involves pre-stretching of the active muscles before executing a vigorous, explosive movement that contracts the muscles involved in sprinting. Plyometrics should be used twice weekly as the final workout item, but only by highly conditioned athletes with leg strength scores of at least 2½ times their body weight. Plyometrics and weight training should not be used in the same workout.

10

ANAEROBIC TRAINING

A halfback is tackled from behind by a slower player. A sprinter is passed in the final 10 yards of the race. A baseball player "runs out of steam" and is tagged out at home. A soccer or basketball player is beat to the ball by a slower player. A tennis player fails to reach a drop shot or cover a lob late in the third set. All are examples of poor anaerobic conditioning that caused a player to either "slow down" or fail to accelerate and approach maximum speed due to fatigue. In most sports, a player is called on to make repetitive short bursts of speed. Ideally, the fourth or fifth burst is run as fast as the first. This is often not the case due to poor anaerobic endurance. The athlete with high anaerobic fitness has the advantages of being able to make these repeated short sprints with minimum rest all at the same high speed, reaching maximum speed more quickly, and holding maximum speed for a longer distance before slowing occurs. You can determine your need for anaerobic training by completing one of the anaerobic tests described in Appendix A.

The physiology of anaerobics and the principles of a sound program to train the anaerobic energy system were discussed in Chapter 5. This chapter applies these principles and is devoted to the improvement of anaerobic fitness through the use of a number of different programs to provide you with a "frest start" on each short sprint in your sport. It may also make you the player who is doing the catching. It is a vital training phase for athletes in all team and individual sports. It is the phase that can give you the "edge."

Anaerobic Training Programs

Pickup Sprints

Pickup sprints involve a gradual increase from a jog to a striding pace, to a maximum effort sprint. A 1-1 ratio of the distance and recovery walk that follows each repetition should be used. Thus, an athlete may jog 50 yards, stride 50, sprint 50, and end that repetition with a 50-yard walk. The walk or slow jog should allow some recovery prior to the next repetition. This jog-stride-sprint-recovery cycle tends to develop speed and reduce the probablility of muscle injury in cold weather.

The above stated cycle is an example of early season training with the exact number of repetitions dependent upon your conditioning level. As conditioning improves, the distance is lengthened with late season pickup sprints reaching segments of 120 yards. It is important to note that use of 120-yard segments involves over-distance training for athletes in most team sports.

New Zealand athletes use a routine similar to pickup sprints involving a series of four 50-yard sprints at near maximum speed (6-7 seconds) per 440-yard lap, jogging for 10-12 seconds after each sprint, and completing

Week	Workout Item	Repetitions	Rest Interval
1	Jog 25 yards, stride 25 yards (³/₄ speed), sprint 25 yards and walk 25 yards	3-5 (add 1 per workout)	No rest between repetitions; walking phase serves as recovery
2	Same as above	6-8 (add 1 per workout)	Same as above
3	Jog 50, stride 50, sprint 50, walk 50	3-5 (add 1 per workout)	Same as above
4	Jog 75, stride 75, sprint 75, walk 75	3-5 (add 1 per workout)	Same as above
5	Jog 75, stride 75, sprint 75, walk 75	6-8 (add 1 per workout)	Same as above
6	Jog 75, stride 75, sprint 75, walk 75	Maximum possible	Same as above

If the workout is not strenuous enough, lengthen the distances, working up to 120, 150, 220 and 300 yard cycles.

Table 10.1. Pickup Sprint Training Program

the 440-yard run in 64-76 seconds. Athletes have performed as many as 50 sprints (12½ X 440) with little reduction in speed on any repetition.

As the repetition distance approaches and exceeds 120 yards (150, 220, 300, 440) anaerobic endurance or lactic acid tolerance is improved. Use of the longer distances should occupy some of the training time for athletes in team sports.

Hollow Sprints

Hollow sprints involve use of two sprints interrupted by a hollow period of recovery such as walking or jogging. One repetition may include a 40 yard sprint, 40-yard jog, 40-yard sprint, and a 40-yard walk for recovery. Similar segments of 80, 120, 150, 220 and 300 yards might be used.

Week	Workout Item	Repetitions	Rest Interval
1	Sprint 25 yards, jog 25 yards, sprint 25 yards and walk 25 yards	3-5 (add 1 per workout)	No rest between repetitions; walk for recovery
2	Same as above	6-8 (add 1 per workout)	Same as above
3	Sprint 50, jog 50, sprint 50, walk 50	3-5 (add 1 per workout)	Same as above
4	Sprint 75, jog 75, sprint 75, walk 75	3-5 (add 1 per workout)	Same as above
5	Same as above	6-8 (add 1 per workout)	Same as above
6	Same as above	Maximum Possible	Same as above

If the workout is not strenuous enough, lengthen the distance, working up to 120, 150, 220, and 300 yard cycles.

Table 10.2 Hollow Sprint Training Program

Interval Sprint Training

Interval training was derived from Fartlek running and has, since the early 1950's, become a popular approach to the training of sprinters. Wind sprints, alternates, and other similar programs are commonly used by

Table 10.3 Interval Sprint Training Program

Workout	Distance	Speed	Repetitions	Interval	Action During Rest Interval
Competive Season:					
1	80 yards	100%	4-6	5-7 minutes	Walk
	150 yards	85%	1-2	10-12 minutes	Walk
2	110 yards Starts on turn from 220 stagger	100%	4-6	8-10 minutes	Walk
	330	100%	1-2	15-20 minutes	Walk
3	160 yards	100%	1	Complete recovery	
					Walk
	80 yards	100%	1		
	90 yards	100%	1		
	100 yards	100%	1		
	110 yards	100%	1		
	120 yards	100%	1		
4	60 yards Starts	100%	6-8	Complete	Walk
5	Easy stretching, calisthenics, relaxed running from 50-150 on grass				
Post Season:					
1	150-220 uphill	75%	8-10	150-220	Walk
2	4-6 miles	Steady jog with no stopping			
3	30, 40, 50, 60, 50, 40, 30 seconds on grass	75%	6	Near complete recovery	Jog-Walk
4	220 differential running, first 220 stride, second 220 hard	50-85%	4	220	Walk
5	4-6 miles	Steady jog with no stopping			
Pre-Season:					
1	550 yards	Best 440 time + 15-20 sec.	2-3	8-10 minutes	Walk
2	4-6 miles	Slow jog mixed with sharp pickups of 50-300 yards. Number of repetitions and rest interval up to the athlete.			
3	330	Best effort + 3-5 sec.	3-5	550 6-8 minutes	Walk
4	150	Best effort + 2-3 sec.	6-8	150 4-6 minutes	Walk
5	110	Maximum with relaxation	10-15	110 2-5 minutes	Walk

Prepared by Glenn Hayes, Track Coach, Virginia Polytechnic Institute.

coaches of football, soccer, baseball, rugby and basketball. These approaches differ from interval sprint training since they possess little formal structure and only a limited attempt to control variables for systematic increases in training intensity. Interval training, on the other hand, has great application to the training of the anaerobic energy system when variables are altered to meet this training objective.

Interval sprint training also differs from that used for training middle and long distance runners. A faster pace ($9/10$ to maximum) and shorter distances (no greater than 440 yards) are used with even shorter distances (under 120 yards) forming the foundation of speed work and anaerobic training. Thus, speed and anaerobic endurance are improved by manipulating the repetition distance, speed, and the recovery action and length. In general, a 1-1 ratio of repetition distance and recovery distance (consuming 2-3 times more time) is preferred.

The basic variables that must be carefully controlled are: frequency of training sessions, length and intensity of each repetition, and length and intensity of the rest interval.

Frequency of Training Sessions. Adequate recovery time is necessary prior to repeating exercise if the body is to fully recover and benefit from the previous workout. Most athletes train daily using 1-2 rest days at the end of the week or just prior to competition during the season. For the team sport athlete, three anaerobic training sessions weekly is sufficient.

Length and Intensity of the Work Interval. There is no magic formula for determining the number and length of repetitions. Training remains an individual matter with this prescription phase determined by the coach and athlete. It is not unreasonable, however, for an athlete to complete 5-50 repetitions of a distance, interspersed with walk-jog recovery periods.

The intensity of training (speed of each repetition) is more important than the length of the workout. In fact, when a training plateau is reached (conditioning level is not changing), improvement occurs by increasing the speed of each repetition without changing the length of the training session.

Length and Intensity of the Rest Interval. It is during the rest interval that the heart adapts to the stress of exercise. Although complete recovery does not occur during the rest interval, partial return to pre-exercise levels does occur. The recovery interval between repetitions allows you to perform much greater exercise volume of high intensity than would normally be possible. This interval is vital to improved conditioning and must be carefully controlled.

A rest/work ratio of 1-1 is suggested between the repetition distance and the recovery walk or jog.

Speed of Each Repetition. For best results, sprints for distances up to 100 yards should take place at maximum or near maximum speed. A pace slower than $^9/_{10}$ speed will not develop a high level of anaerobic fitness.

Specificity of Interval Sprint Training. Work and intensity of each repetition should simulate competitive conditions except when overdistance training is used.

Maximum Effort Training

Maximum effort training is an excellent method of improving the anaerobic energy system by completly exhausting the athlete in all-out efforts at the end of a training session. Only the best mentally and physically conditioned athletes will be capable of using this type of training. Maximum effort training is one of the few good methods of equalizing exercise effort among athletes at different conditioning levels. It offers training geared to the individual with each working against his own previous distance or time record, each coping with his own stress and psychological barriers, until finally only complete physical exhaustion causes cessation of exercise.

Maximum effort sessions should be used 1-2 times weekly at the end of the workout. Records should be kept and periodic testing used to determine individual progress.

The basic program is as follows:

- All-out Sprint—perform an all out sprint at maximum speed until no longer able to continue. Record the distance.
- Distance Hop—Perform a one-legged hop at maximum speed until no longer able to continue. Record the distance and time. Repeat using the opposite leg.
- Squat Jumps—Perform a maximum number of squat jumps, falling to a right angle only and avoiding the full-squat position, in a period of 90 seconds. Slowly increase the time limit as progress occurs.

Squat Jumps

These basic exercises can be supplemented by Concentrations I and II shown below to provide variety and intensity to the lower torso and muscles affecting sprinting.

Concentration I:

- Running in Place—Lift the knees to waist level, sprint in place until no longer able to continue. Record the time. Avoid pacing or barely lifting the feet from the ground.
- Treadmill Pacing—Set the treadmill at 15 mph to develop anaerobic endurance and run until you can no longer continue.
- 300-Yard Run—Record the time in a 300-yard sprint.
- Two-legged Hop—Record the distance covered in 45 seconds. Slowly increase the time limit.

Sprinting-in-place to exhaustion

Concentration II:

- 440-Yard Dash Plus—Surprise runners at the finish of 440-yard dash with the command to continue sprinting as far as possible.
- Bench Jump—Stand parallel to a bench; jump to the other side with a two-foot take-off, immediately jumping back to the starting position. Repeat this action until you are no longer able to continue. Record the total number of jumps.
- Isometric Charge–with the legs moving continuously and shoulder and hands placed against an immovable object (sled, wall, post), continue to drive forward until no longer able to continue.

Summary

Quick energy stores provide the fuel for short sprints. A high level of anaerobic conditioning will help you reach maximum speed sooner, hold maximum speed longer, slow less at the end of the racing distance, and recover faster after a short sprint to perform another with limited reduction in speed due to fatigue. Pickup sprints, hollow sprints, interval sprint training and maximum effort training are all effective programs for the development of the anaerobic energy system. These programs are used to condition the anaerobic system, not to make you a faster runner. With a high level of conditioning, however, you will be able to sprint repeated short distances in your sport all at the same high speed. Unlike traditional wind sprints used by some coaches, accurate records are kept (distance run, speed, length of the rest interval, action during the rest interval) to make certain you do more work per unit of time each training session. Sample programs of champion sprinters are shown in Appendix E.

11
FORM
TRAINING

Sprinting style varies from individual to individual; so-called correct form is associated with championship caliber sprinters. It is, however, a dangerous practice to duplicate the form of champions without careful analysis of your specific characteristics and style. There is no perfect style suitable for individuals of all body types, height, weight, size of levers, and differences in strength, flexibility, power, and agility. One factor is very evident, however; fast sprinters can be distinguished from slow sprinters through a number of characteristics of which form is an important aspect.

It becomes evident that absolutes of ideal form do not exist. It is the purpose of this chapter to present the commonly accepted principles and styles of starting and sprinting that will assist you in developing your speed to its maximum potential for your sport.

The Unnatural Act Of Sprinting

Although running is one of the basic fundamental movements, efficient form is far from a natural act. Team sports and free play do little to develop proper form. One has only to observe the multitude of faulty styles at the pre-school, elementary, high school, and college level to confirm the complexity and difficulty of its mastery. It therefore requires special attention to eliminate faulty habits as early as possible through formalized form training. As you move closer to championship caliber, speed improvement becomes more difficult and the "little things," such as minute details of correct form, become more important. A careful analysis of all three phases of sprinting (start, middle phase, and finish) will help you reach your full potential.

The Start

Although the information in this section is written for the track sprinter, it has great application to football players as well as athletes in basketball, baseball, soccer, field hockey, rugby, lacrosse, and racket sports. If you are an athlete in one of these sports, pay close attention to foot spacing and the action of the arms and legs and forward lean during acceleration.

There are three basic starts named according to the distance between the feet in the starting blocks: the *elongated, medium*, and *bunch*. In all three styles, the front foot is placed 14-21" behind the starting line. Back foot placement varies. The *elongated start* is assumed by preparing the block for the front foot and then extending the rear leg until the knee is even with the heel of the front foot. The *medium start* is assumed by placing the knee of the rear leg almost even with the toe of the front foot. The *bunch start* is assumed by placing the toe of the rear foot about one foot behind the heel of the front foot. Obviously, spacing between the feet varies for the three types of starts: elongated (21-26"), medium (16-21") and bunch (11-12"). Additional guidelines are offered for determining spacing in the commonly used medium start and its variations:
- The rear foot should be as close to the starting line as possible. A rear leg angle of 120° and a front angle of 90° in the set position is desirable.
- The back should slope slightly downward toward the shoulder.
- The lead foot should be placed about 1' from the line. The knee of the rear leg is now placed opposite the center of the lead foot.

A fourth starting style has evolved and gained popularity following its use by Armin Hary of Germany in his 100-meter victory in the 1980 Olympic Games. At the second step of the race Hary was well ahead of the field. Outstanding track and field authority, Lloyd C. Bud Winter describes the *Rocket Sprint Start* by pointing out the differences between this method and the medium start:
- Foot spacing—the front block is further back from the starting line (28") as is the rear block (33").
- At the command Come to your Marks—weight is back with arms, neck and back relaxed. Arms slant backward from the starting line and the head is down with eyes looking between the arms.

- At the command Get Set—the head is up and eyes focused 3' ahead, weight is shifted slowly forward, then up. The front knee is lifted 6-8" with legs almost parallel to the ground. The buttocks are about 3" higher than the shoulders. A slow shift forward places tension on the hands for limited time only.
- At the command Go—the left arm drives long and forward while the right is driven back to the hip only, then thrust forward. The head is up with eyes focused on the finish tape. The drive angle is low and forward. The lead knee is high with the first step touching 16-19" beyond the starting line.
- Pickup after block clearing—steps are long, knee lift remains high, and arms are thrust long and forward.

What Research Says. Research provides additional insight into the most efficient style. A summary of findings follows:

Reaction Time (RT) and Acceleration:
- It takes approximately 0.1 seconds to respond to the gun and an additional 0.5 seconds to clear the blocks.
- About 90 percent of maximum acceleration occurs within 15 yards with 95 percent velocity attained at 20 yards and maximum speed at about 60 yards depending upon your conditioning level.
- RT is not related to block spacing.

Foot and Hand Spacing:
- Wide variations in distances are effective.
  a. Runners with long legs should place their forward foot a greater distance from the lead hand.
  b. A 16-21" distance between the blocks appears to be the most effective spacing.
  c. The 26" spacing produces greater velocity in clearing the blocks; however, the advantage is lost within ten yards.
  d. Times are improved in a 10- and 30-yard dash using the medium start when the hands and lead foot are placed as close to the starting line as feasible.
  e. Narrow hand spacing (8" between thumbs) may produce faster acceleration to maximum speed.

Comparison of the Three Basic Starts:
- The bunch start is more conducive to high hip elevation, improved forward truck lean, and more rapid leg movements.
- The bunch start allows you to clear the blocks sooner but with less velocity than from a medium stance. For shorter 2-5 yard sprints, the bunch start appears quicker (quick dive play in football); however, times may not be as fast should the distance be greater.
- The medium start position is significantly faster for runs from 10-50

yards than the elongated and bunch styles.
• The elongated stance produces greater velocity as the runner vacates the blocks; however, after a 10-yard distance, no advantage remains.

Basic Starts in Track

Bunch Start

Medium Start

Elongated Start

Force Against the Blocks:
- Top - class sprinters exert block force with both feet at the same time.
- Strong rear leg action is characteristic of better starts.
- The greatest amount of force is placed on the rear leg, however, the lead leg is in contact with the block for a greater time and contributes more to block velocity.
- The angle of the rear knee affects force against the rear block. At 180° the rear knee and hip extensors exert little rear block force.
- Force against the blocks will vary according to body weight, experience, knee angle and spacing.
- A 20″ spread produced a total block force of 386 lbs. and an 11″ spread produced 346 lbs.
- In comparing block pressure with foot spacing, the elongated start provided the most powerful force: 26" spread–404 lb., 20″ spread–386 lb., 11″ spread–346 lb., and a 16″ spread–303 lb.
- Block force does not guarantee a rapid start and rapid acceleration which may be more closely tied to body lean, angle of the legs, and center of gravity.

Angle:
- A knee angle of 80° was significantly slower than angles of 90° and 135° from 0-10 yards and 0-30 yards.
- A rear joint angle of 165° (medium spacing) that elevates the hips improved 50-yard dash times.

Length of the Hold:

- RT to the gun is improved when the stimulus can be anticipated. Rhythmic digit starting in football, for example, yields faster RT than nonrhythmic signals.
- The optimum time of holding sprinters by starters is 1.5 - 2.0 seconds. Some starters are surprisingly consistent in their "hold" time as determined by observation. With the new automatic timing devices in use in international competition, an anticipated response or moving "with the gun" is impossible and considered a "break."

The Start (for the Football Player)

Football players can learn a great deal from the preceding discussion on track starts concerning foot spacing, weight distribution, length of first several steps, arm and leg action, and forward lean. The medium start and its spacing is best suited for adaptation to the three or four point stance in football. The bunch start spacing is helpful for a quick dive play to help you reach the open hole sooner.

Since the "snap signal" is known and can be anticipated, reaction time is much less important. The key is to assume the proper three or four point stance and explode forward or laterally with a rather short first step, good body lean, and a powerful upward thrust of the knee and opposite arm. Practice using different foot spacings for the medium start until you find the combination best suited for you.

Proper three - and four-point stances for football.

Four-point stance

Three-point stance

The Start (for other Sports)

Athletes in basketball, soccer, field hockey, rugby, lacrosse, tennis, and baseball generally accelerate into near full sprinting speed from a moving position; rarely from a standstill. These athletes should concentrate on the form-related items in the next section dealing with the "middle phase" of sprinting (acceleration to maximum speed). Often, acceleration occurs after a firm plant of one foot and a sprint in the opposite direction. Such an action does require proper forward lean, a short first step, and form similar to that described for the first 5-8 yards of a 100-yard dash.

Training to Improve the Start and Acceleration
Training in this area revolves around four basic components .

Reaction Time (RT) can be significantly improved through weight training, calisthenics, and specific drills such as sprint starts that simulate actual race or game movements. Total body and lower torso RT are the key areas for sprinting. To improve RT, you should concentrate on strength/power training exercises that reproduce the action coming from the blocks, find your ideal starting form (keeping in mind that holding the "get set" posture for more than one second will hinder your RT), study and time starters at each meet to improve your anticipation response to the gun, and learn to concentrate on the first muscular movement forward from the blocks or from your three or four point stance rather than the sound of the gun or signal (which you can't help but hear). Additional specific exercises to improve RT include daily practice in starts and sprints 25-40 yards (with a gun), use of the mountain climber exercise (pushup position with one leg forward; on "go," legs make one change and stop; responding to commands of an assistant) and the forward dive exercise (from a standing position, runners dive forward as far as possible on the command "go").

Speed of Arm and Leg Movement can be improved through sprint-assisted training and strength/power training (see Chapters 7 and 8).

The Force of the Legs Against the Blocks can be improved through strength/power training. The "greyhound effect" of stepping onto a high speed treadmill with a treadbelt speed of over 20 mph produces acceleration to near maximum speed in 1-2 seconds and is an effective method of improving acceleration.

Starting Form can be improved through mastery of the most efficient starting style for you and periodic practice as discussed in this chapter.

The Middle Phase

There is no reduction in speed during this part of a sprint; however, the power used in the start is replaced by a more relaxed movement as full speed is reached. A sprinter reaches maximum speed in about 6 seconds and is capable of holding this pace for 15-20 yards before slowing. During this phase, coasting occurs through a reduction in tension and adequate

The plant and sprint commonly used in team sports.

striding without a fighting effort. Long, smooth striding as well as suffi- cient strength and power aid in improving the coasting phase. Relaxation is essential after maximum speed is reached. In sprinting, the muscle groups involved in each stride undergo a lightning fast switch from contraction to relaxation. The sprinter's secret is the ability to make this switch skillfully and to maintain a relaxed style of running without de- creasing the force of the drive. Proper form described during the "Middle Phase" was extracted from the literature of numerous experts in sprint- ing.

Body Position:

- The body gradually reaches its proper running posture at 15-20 yards and may be nearly upright or leaning as much as 24-25° depending upon individual style. The actual degree of lean is dependent upon wind resistance and rate of acceleration. Too much lean prevents a full stride, while an overly vertical position diminishes forward drive.
- The eyes are kept straight ahead, focusing on the track or field from 25 yards ahead to the finish line.
- The head is held in a natural position, the facial muscles are relaxed and the chest is firm and open to give the impression of running with the chest as a shield.

Leg Action:

- Knee lift reaches the level of the hip to secure maximum length of stride in an up-and-out motion. Rear "kickup" of the foot should bring the heel just to the edge of the buttocks.
- The leg movement is always a pushing and not a pulling motion; therefore, the center of gravity must be in front of the planted foot.
- The foot first contacts the ground on the outside edge of the sole high on the ball of the foot (joints of the little toe). Then, a riding onto the full sole occurs as the foot is planted, causing the heel to lower (contro- versy exists as to whether it actually touches the ground).
- The toes are pointed straight ahead both during the power and the recovery phase.
- There is a resilient bounce from the balls of the feet, produced by a final flip of the toes as the foot leaves the surface. At ground/toe contact, the knee is flexed and the ankles relaxed to permit upward spring and start of another cycle in the series of jumps characterized as sprinting. Driving time is shortened by pulling the toes upward toward the knee immediately after ground contact occurs. Also, the more weight that is placed on the driving leg, the greater the driving force against the

surface. Complete extension of the leg at pushoff does not occur because of the limited time the foot is in contact with the ground. At maximum speed, support time (ground contact) and non-support time (body is in the air) is approximately equal among good sprinters.

Arm Action:

- The best arm action for a sprinter is one in which the movement is directly backwards and forwards from the shoulders, with the elbows close to the side. The arm acts independently of the shoulders, as though the upper arm were connected by a pin to the shoulder and free to move as on a toy doll. The angle of the elbow is slightly greater than 90° so that the hand in the backward movement travels beyond the hip. The action matches the leg action in force and range of movement. The arms actually lead the legs, and a high-quality leg drive is only possible when arm action is in tune with it.
- The maximum range of movement of the hands is from a point near the height of the shoulder to a point out from the ilium. The hands do not swing so far that they pass behind the body. Forward arm action never continues above the shoulders nor backward more than 6-8″ beyond the hip.
- The hands are held as naturally as possible in a half closed manner.

Proper sprinting form

The Finish

There are three basic types of finishes: *straight running form*, *the shrug*, and the *lunge*. Most experts feel than any change in proper running form as you approach the finish line will detract from forward propulsion and decrease speed. Therefore, straight running form to a point several feet beyond the finish tape appears to be mechanically desirable. Not all sprinters subscribe to this theory and contend that an advantage is gained by shrugging the shoulders, lunging or even turning as they approach the finish line.

The finish

Training for the Improvement of Form

In general, form improvement requires use of numerous methods and resources:
* Knowledge of correct form as indicated in this chapter, on films, and by your coach.
* Use of film or video tape to analyze form and identify faulty style. Style deviations compatible with individual body type are not altered. The principle of individual differences is recognized and unnecessary "patterning" after other athletes is avoided.

Common Areas of Difficulty	Correction
Arm action	Practice loose, swinging movements from a standing position. Swing entire arm from the shoulders. Thumbs should brush the thighs. Increase arm speed, elbows more flexed, hands loosely cupped, brushing thumbs against the side. Repeat while moving forward high on the toes.
Hands too low	Place tape around the wrist and over the neck.
Hands moving too far forward	Practice arm swing to contact coach's hands when standing behind the runner.
Hands outside line of elbows	Sprint while holding a stick in both hands with proper spacing. Using tape on both wrists at proper spacing.
Body lean	Practice sprinting with eye concentration on a fixed spot, either high or low, depending upon the problem. Discuss mechanics of proper lean at maximum speed.
Incorrect head alignment	Same as above.
Limited foot bounce	Walk forward high on toes using proper arm action, body weight as low as possible, bounce the knee forward from the foot. Stand on one foot, bounce opposite foot up and down on the sole as rapidly as possible.
Unnecessary pounding into the ground	Practice running as lightly as possible with correct foot-ground contact.
Incorrect knee-leg action	Practice running upstairs two at a time and running along the beach in shallow water.
Striding: Overstriding	Practice running along the beach in shallow water. Avoid placing the lead foot beyond the center of gravity.
Understriding	Concentrate on complete extension of the hip and knee joint at ground contact and complete knee pickup of the recovery leg. See section on stride training.
Upper arm tension	Unclench the fist and generate tension in the thumb with pressure against the index finger.
Neck/facial tension	Roll out the lower lip and yawn.

Table 11.1 Common form areas and their correction.

• Examination of footprints in the cinders for stride length, consistency of stride over the racing distance, depth of the impression of the ball of the foot, absence of a cinder trail behind the foot marks, and direction of the toe at contact.

Table 11.1 identifies some of the more common form faults and suggests ways to correct the problem. The following additional drills are suggested for form improvement:

Stride Running—begin with a walk, slowly progressing to maximum speed in several repetitions. From a standing position, rise up on the toe of one leg. While high on the toe, reach out with the other leg and snap that lead leg down to the ground. When the lead leg contacts the ground, spring forward off the toe and continue sprinting with this exaggerated stride as you try to touch each 5-yard marker with the left foot.

Foreleg Reach—use a long reach each step.

Knee Lift—run in place, knees high, move down the track at 2 mph; walk the turns.

Toe Running—run in place high on the toes, lean forward and sprint straight ahead.

Low Hurdling—force overstriding with hurdles.

Arm Reach—from a low stride running with a partner, exaggerate arm reach without accelerating. Note your speed compared to your partner.

Relaxation Striding—sprint with a loose jaw and hands.

Jumping Strides—increase stride length until you are actually jumping each step.

Common Form Errors.

Cross-cutting with arms

Neck/facial tension

Elbows too far from body

**Improper head position
and body lean**

Summary

Sprinting style varies from athlete to athlete, with so-called correct form associated with champion sprinters. Actually, there is no perfect style designed for athletes of all body types, height, weight, lever sizes and differences in strength/power, flexibility and agility. It is a fact, however, that form is important if specfic faults are restricting you from taking your optimum stride and stride rate. Use of the commonly accepted form described in this chapter guarantees proper action in all major areas.

Modern-day sprinting form may not be so modern. Sprinters are portrayed on Greek vases with runners well up on their toes, knees lifted high, bodies erect, and arms swinging vigorously. These same factors are stressed by modern day coaches. Until recently, little has been written about "how to run faster." Archie Hahn's Book, *How to Sprint*, published in 1925, stands with a brief book by Lloyd Winter, *So You Want to be a Sprinter*, and four books by Dintiman, *Sprinting Speed: Its Improvement for Major Sports Competition* (1971), *What Research Tells the Coach about Sprinting* (1974), *How to Run Faster: Step-by-Step Instructions on How to Increase Foot Speed* (1984) as the only texts ever written that deal entirely with sprinting.

APPENDICES

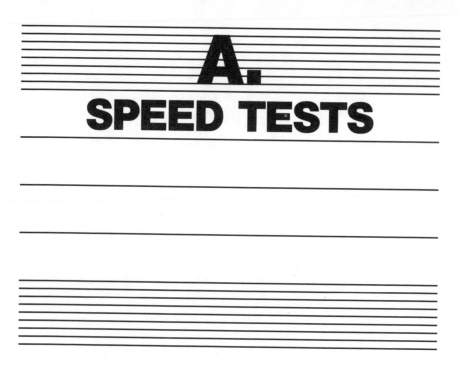

A.
SPEED TESTS

40-Yard Dash (Stationary Start)

Equipment: Stop watches (1-3), finish tape (yarn)
Reliability: 0.89-0.91
Procedure: Assume a stationary start (3 point football or track stance) and respond to the commands: "runners to your mark, get set, go." Timers are placed at the finish line and start their watches on the command "Go" or with the sight of smoke from a starter's gun. A 40-yard dash is used by professional football teams with the test conducted in this manner.

40-, 50-, 100-, 300- and 440-Yard Dash (Flying Start)

Equipment: Stop watches (1-3), finish tape (yarn)
Reliability: 0.87-0.92
Procedure: A 15-yard running start is allowed to eliminate reaction time and starting ability. Subjects reach full running stride prior to arrival to the "starting tape" where timers start their watches. As the finish tape is touched, a white flag (folded on top of the tape) falls, keying the timers to stop their watches. The best of two trials is recorded in your personal

record sheet for distances up to 100 yards. Only one trial is used for the 300- and 440- yard dash. A 15-minute formal warm up period is used before the test and a 10-minute rest period between the first and second trials.

Anaerobic Capacity

Equipment: Stop watches (1-3), finish tape (yarn)
Procedure: Method One: determine your 50-yard and 100-yard time (flying start). Double your 50-yard time. This figure should be more than 0.2 of a second less than the 100-yard time. **Method Two:** determine your 100-yard and 300-yard time from a stationary start. Triple your 100 time. This time should be no more than 3-5 seconds less than your 300-yard time. A sprinter who can complete 300 yards in less than 31 seconds is ready for national competition in the 100 and 200 meter races; 33-34 seconds for lesser caliber competition. **Method Three:** an athlete with high anaerobic fitness should be capable of performing a respectable 440-yard dash at a pace approximately five times his best 100-yard effort.

100-yard time	440-yard target
9.0	45.0
9.5	47.5
10.0	50.0
10.5	52.5
11.0	55.0
11.5	57.5
12.0	60.0

Stride Length

Equipment: Tape measure, smooth track or surface that will leave a footprint.
Procedure: The best stride guideline for men is 1.14 X height plus or minus 4 inches (under age 16) or 1.265 X height (17 or older) and for women is 1.15 X height.

EXAMPLE: Tom Hughes, age 18, 6'0"
Optimal stride = 1.265 X 72" or 91 inches
Lynne Rose, age 18, 5'9"
Optimal stride = 1.15 X 69" or 79 inches

Place two markers 25 yards apart on a cinder track. Step off 50 yards from the first marker, making this the starting line. Begin running from this mark, accelerating to maximum speed just prior to reaching the 25-yard area where you have smoothed out the surface. Note the prints on the track. Measure the two longest strides from the tip of the rear toe (front of mark) to the tip of the front toe.

Stride Rate

Equipment: Stop watches (1-3) or video tape, finish tape (yarn)
Reliability: 0.88
Procedure: Complete one trial of the 40-yard dash (flying start) as described previously. Ask your coach to videotape your run; play it back in slow motion and count the number of steps per second. An alternate method is to ask someone to count "one" each time your left foot hits the ground. Your left foot should make contact with the starting line; counting begins the next time your left foot strikes the surface. Multiply the final count by two and observe which foot hits the ground at the finish line. If the right foot made ground contact, only one step is added.

EXAMPLE: John Hurst: 40-yard time = 4.8, Total steps for the entire distance = 22. Stride rate = 22 divided by 4.8 or 4.58 per second.

40-yard Dash with a Flying Start

B.

TESTS OF STRENGTH, FLEXIBILITY AND BODY FAT

Upper Body Strength (Bench Press)

Equipment: Free weights and bench rack, Universal Gym or Nautilus
Procedure: Assume the bench press position described in Chapter 8, Table 8.1. Your task is to locate your 1RM or the amount of weight you can press one time through trial and error. Estimate your maximum lift and attempt one trial. After a 5-minute rest period, add or remove weight, depending upon the outcome of the first trial, and press the new weight. If the weight can be lifted more than once, you again rest five minutes before making another attempt with additional weight.

Your minimum standard is 1 X body weight. If you weigh 175 pounds, you should strive to bench press 175 pounds.

Dynamic Leg Strength (Universal Gym or Nautilus)

Equipment: Universal Gym or Nautilus
Procedure: Adjust the seat position until your legs are bent at right angles (90°). Experiment in one of your workouts to locate the approximate

amount of weight you can leg press one time. On the following workout, add 10 pounds to the amount you identified and attempt to press that weight one time. If you are successful, wait five minutes and repeat the test after you have added 10-20 pounds. If you are unsuccessful, adjust the weight downward and repeat the test. You should try to locate the exact amount of weight you can leg press one time in only two attempts (1RM).

Your minimum standard is 2½ X body weight. If you weigh 150 pounds, you should strive to leg press 375 pounds.

Static Leg Strength (Dynamometer)

Equipment: Leg dynamometer calibrated from 0 to 2,500 pounds, chain 24 inches long to attach to a hook in the center of a 24″ handle, base for the attachment of the dynamometer, and a meter stick fixed at exactly 119°.
Reliability: 0.88-0.92
Procedure: Stand erect in the foot placement markings holding the bar in the center with both palms down. Place the bar at the junction of your

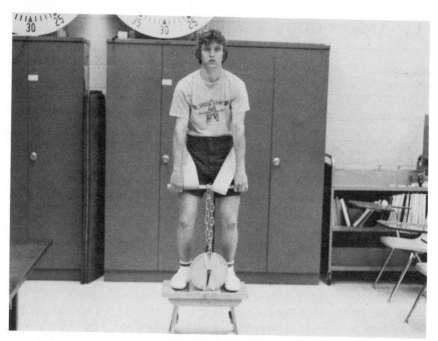

Static Leg Strength Test

thighs and trunk and attach the belt as low as possible over your hips and onto the handle. Grasp the dynamometer chain and flex both knees until an angle of 119° is obtained on the meter stick. Connect the chain to the handle. Drive your legs downward as hard as possible as you pull upward with both hands. The legs should be nearly straight at the end of the lift. The head should be up and the back kept straight at all times. The best of three attempts is recorded.

Your minimum standard is 6 X body weight. If you weigh 150 pounds, you should strive to leg press 900 pounds.

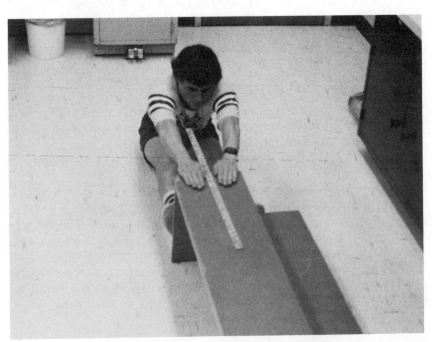

Sit-and-Reach Test to Measure Trunk Flexion

Flexibility (the Sit-and-Reach Test)

Equipment: A bench with a measuring stick extending 15″ over the front edge toward the subject being measured.

Procedure: Sit on the floor with your knees together and feet flat against the measuring bench. Reach forward slowly (no warmup is permitted) as far as possible with the arms fully extended, keeping the knees locked. The best of three trials is recorded.

Your minimum standard is 20-24 inches.

Measurement of Body Fat

Weight Charts: Avoid the use of weight charts to determine your desirable body weight and body fat. These charts have a number of pitfalls: a) it is possible to be within the range of suggested weight and still be overweight; b) it is possible to be classified as overweight or obese (10-20 lbs. above suggested ranges) when you are at a desirable weight and possess little fatty tissue; c) some charts allow you to gain weight with age, suggesting it is fine to be fat at age 30, 40, or 50 when, in actuality, weight should decrease with age: weighing the same at age 40 as you did at age 20 probably means you are fat, due to a higher ratio of fat to muscle mass; d) the three categories of small, medium and large frame encourage cheating; and e) the key to obesity is not total body weight but total body fat, and weight charts DO NOT reveal the presence of fat.

Skinfold Measures: Skinfold measures are the most practical method of determining your percent of body fat. Since one-half of all fat lies just under the skin, using fat calipers or pinching the skin between the thumb and index finger can identify fat tissue. A deep pinch in the midsection while lying on your back that measures more than 1″ indicates excessive fat in this area.

Fat calipers precisely measuring in millimeters the back of the upper arm and the supra-iliac can accurately predict the percentage of total body fat. If you do not have fat calipers, borrow any type of calipers that measure the thickness of wood in millimeters such as the Executive Pocket Chum available in hardware stores, or the practical, inexpensive ($9.95) Fat-o-Meter complete with illustrations and norms (Write: Health and Education Services, 2442 Irving Park Rd., Chicago, Illinois 60618). To determine your body fat classification, use one of the following approaches for boys and girls or men and women:

Boys and Girls (ages 6-18):

Triceps. Stand erect with arms hanging to sides. Partner takes a deep pinch (between thumb and index finger) on the back of the upper arm, halfway between the shoulder and elbow. You can now flex your arm and relax again to assure partner that he or she is pinching fat only and not muscle mass. The calipers are placed 1/16 inch below the pinch. Record the average of three measurements.

Use the percentile norm charts to determine your catagory. In general, the following interpretations can be made: 15th percentile or below = VERY THIN; 16th-30th percentile = THIN; 31-60th percentile = AVERAGE; 61-75th percentile = PLUMP; above 75th percentile = OBESE.

Triceps Skinfold Measures of Youth by Sex and Age at Last Birthday.

Sex and age	n	5th	10th	Percentile 25th	50th	75th	90th	95th
Male		In millimeters						
12 years	643	5.1	5.5	6.8	9.4	13.3	19.6	23.3
13 years	626	4.5	5.2	6.7	9.1	12.9	19.3	22.6
14 years	617	4.2	4.7	6.0	7.8	12.0	17.1	20.8
15 years	613	4.3	4.7	5.8	7.6	10.7	15.8	20.7
16 years	555	4.2	4.7	5.8	7.5	11.1	15.8	20.2
17 years	489	4.1	4.6	5.5	7.5	11.4	15.6	20.5
Female								
12 years	547	6.1	7.0	8.8	11.8	16.0	22.2	25.2
13 years	582	6.4	7.3	9.2	12.4	17.1	22.8	25.5
14 years	586	7.1	8.3	10.7	14.0	18.5	23.3	26.7
15 years	502	7.4	8.6	11.6	14.8	19.5	25.1	29.4
16 years	535	7.7	9.2	11.8	15.6	20.8	25.5	29.7
17 years	468	8.1	9.6	12.1	15.8	20.5	25.0	29.1

n = sample size; X = mean

DHEW PUBLICATION NO. (HSM) 73-1602; U.S. DEPARTMENT OF HEALTH, EDUCATION, AND WELFARE

Measurement of Body Fat.

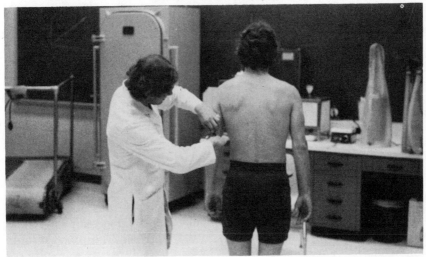

Triceps

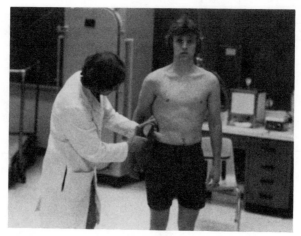

Supra-Iliac

Men and Women (over 18):

Triceps. Same as previously described.

Supra-iliac. Grasp the skin just above the crest of the right ilium (side of body about halfway between hip bone and underarm area). Lift the fold at a slight angle to the vertical along the normal fold line. Place the calipers 1/16 inch under the fold. Record the average of three measurements.

The norm chart below is in milliliters of fat (1 inch equals 25 mm, 1/16 inch equals 1.5 mm). Convert your reading accordingly and estimate your category.

Classification	UPPER ARM Men	Women	SUPRA-ILIAC Men	Women
THIN	1.0-7.0	1.0-10.0	1.0-10.0	1.0-13.0
AVERAGE	7.1-12.0	10.1-20.0	10.1-20.0	13.1-25.0
PLUMP	12.1-20.0	20.1-30.0	20.1-28.0	25.1-33.0
OBESE	20.0 up	30.1 up	29.1 up	33.1 up

In general, average or thin readings in these two areas suggest that you possess a low percentage of body fat. If you fall in the plump and obese classifications in both areas, a diet and exercise program are suggested.

YEAR-ROUND PROGRAM

JANUARY
S	M	T	W	T	F	S
1	2	3	4	5	6	7
8	9	10	11	12	13	14
15	16	17	18	19	20	21
22	23	24	25	26	27	28
29	30	31				

FEBRUARY
S	M	T	W	T	F	S
			1	2	3	4
5	6	7	8	9	10	11
12	13	14	15	16	17	18
19	20	21	22	23	24	25
26	27	28	29			

MARCH
S	M	T	W	T	F	S
				1	2	3
4	5	6	7	8	9	10
11	12	13	14	15	16	17
18	19	20	21	22	23	24
25	26	27	28	29	30	31

APRIL
S	M	T	W	T	F	S
1	2	3	4	5	6	7
8	9	10	11	12	13	14
15	16	17	18	19	20	21
22	23	24	25	26	27	28
29	30					

MAY
S	M	T	W	T	F	S
		1	2	3	4	5
6	7	8	9	10	11	12
13	14	15	16	17	18	19
20	21	22	23	24	25	26
27	28	29	30	31		

JUNE
S	M	T	W	T	F	S
					1	2
3	4	5	6	7	8	9
10	11	12	13	14	15	16
17	18	19	20	21	22	23
24	25	26	27	28	29	30

JULY
S	M	T	W	T	F	S
1	2	3	4	5	6	7
8	9	10	11	12	13	14
15	16	17	18	19	20	21
22	23	24	25	26	27	28
29	30	31				

AUGUST
S	M	T	W	T	F	S
			1	2	3	4
5	6	7	8	9	10	11
12	13	14	15	16	17	18
19	20	21	22	23	24	25
26	27	28	29	30	31	

SEPTEMBER
S	M	T	W	T	F	S
						1
2	3	4	5	6	7	8
9	10	11	12	13	14	15
16	17	18	19	20	21	22
23	24	25	26	27	28	29
30						

OCTOBER
S	M	T	W	T	F	S
	1	2	3	4	5	6
7	8	9	10	11	12	13
14	15	16	17	18	19	20
21	22	23	24	25	26	27
28	29	30	31			

NOVEMBER
S	M	T	W	T	F	S
				1	2	3
4	5	6	7	8	9	10
11	12	13	14	15	16	17
18	19	20	21	22	23	24
25	26	27	28	29	30	

DECEMBER
S	M	T	W	T	F	S
						1
2	3	4	5	6	7	8
9	10	11	12	13	14	15
16	17	18	19	20	21	22
23	24	25	26	27	28	29
30	31					

Master Schedule for a Continuous Training Program

Season	Approximate Time Period	Programs	Comments
Postseason	4½-5 months	Sprint training	Alternate day program involving pickup sprints, hollow sprints, interval sprint training, and some speed play.
		Form and stride training	Twice weekly. Includes starting practice.
		Weight training	Training for effect, three times weekly. Use basic program and concentrations stressing both strength and explosive power training. Great strength gains should occur during this period—to be maintained with one workout weekly during the in-season period.
		Flexibility training	Daily, prior to sprint training and following each weight training session.
		Maximum effort training	Three times weekly using the basic program and concentrations.
Preseason	2-2½ months	Sprint training	Alternate day program including sprint-assisted training (towing, downhill running or treadmill running).
		Form and stride training	Three to four times weekly. Includes starting practice and concentration on weakness areas for perfection.
		Weight training/explosive power training	Alternate day program when not engaged in sprint training. Explosive power training is oriented toward improved starting ability.
		Flexibility training	Daily, prior to sprint training and following each weight training session.
		Maximum effort training	Three times weekly following each sprint training session.
		Reaction-time training	Twice weekly prior to sprint training sessions.
In-season	4-4½ months	Sprint training	Daily, including sprint-assisted training two or three times weekly prior to the competitive season or first contest.
		Form and stride training	Two to three times weekly including starting practice which occurs at the beginning of the practice session when athletes are fresh.
		Weight training or Isometrics	Training for strength maintenance—once weekly (middle of the week) using the basic program, two to three times weekly for additional strength and explosive power improvement prior to the first scheduled contest if needed. Follows sprint training.
		Flexibility training	Daily, prior to sprint training and following each weight training or isometric training session.
		Maximum effort training	Two to three times weekly for five to fifteen minutes following the sprint training session on days when weight training or isometrics are not scheduled. Used only until one to two weeks prior to the first scheduled contest.
		Testing	Fifty-yard dash with a flying start—once weekly.

Football, basketball, soccer, and baseball players should also emphasize skill training in weakness areas during the postseason as a means of improving performance. Less attention should be given to skill areas where competence is already high.

D.

40-YARD DASH REQUIREMENTS OF COLLEGE AND PROFESSIONAL FOOTBALL TEAMS

Short sprints are common in football and combine both reaction and movement time qualities. The most commonly used test of speed in professional and college football is the 40-yard dash,which is used for the purpose of:
- determining the position best suited for the individual,
- evaluating the overall potential of an individual for a specific position,
- determining overall football ability.

Although it is doubtful that a 40-yard dash is an adequate measure of football ability, it does provide valuable information to coaches who have established minimum speed standards for various positions. Failure to meet these standards, experience has strongly indicated, makes it extremely difficult to become an excellent player for that position.

In general, the speed requirements for offensive and defensive personnel fall in the following order (fastest to slowest requirements):

Offensive	*Defensive*
Flankers	Cornerbacks
Halfbacks	Safety
Quarterback	End
Tight End	Corner Linebackers
Fullback	Middle Linebackers
Guard	Tackles
Tackle	

Rarely is a quarterback as fast as the desired requirements listed by some professional teams.

The 40-yard dash standards below include the range of times desired by most professional and university teams.

Professional

Offensive:

Flanker. 4.4-4.6
Halfback 4.5-4.8
Quarterback. 4.7-5.0
Tight End 4.7-5.0
Fullback. 4.7-5.0
Guard. 4.8-5.1
Center 4.8-5.3
Tackle. 4.8-5.4

Defensive:

Cornerback 4.4-4.7
Safety. 4.6-4.8
Corner Linebacker. 4.7-4.9
Middle Linebacker. 4.7-4.9
End. 4.8-5.1
Tackle. 5.0-5.3

University

Backs. 4.7-4.8
Ends. 4.8-4.9
Quarterbacks 4.9
Linemen. 4.9-5.4

Defensive backs 4.6-4.9
Linebackers. 4.8-5.2
Linemen. 4.9-5.5

E.

SAMPLE TRAINING
PROGRAMS OF
CHAMPION
SPRINTERS

Training for the 100- and 200-Meter Dash

Season	Monday 1	Tuesday 2	Wednesday 3	Thursday 4	Friday 5	Saturday 6
November-December—6 workouts weekly alternating easy and hard training. 3½ times indoors and 2½ times outdoors.	Indoors—20 minutes jogging and warmup exercises, 10/12 X 30-40m pickup sprints reaching ¾ speed with 1 minute walk after each. 15-20 X 20-25m easy starts. Walk 10-15 minutes. Medicine ball throwing, low hurdle running over 8 at 3m apart. 10-12 minutes handball plus jogging.	Outdoors—5 minutes jogging and calisthenics. 8-10 X 80-100m pickup runs walking 10-15 minutes after each. Walk 10-12 minutes, 200, 300, 400, and 200m runs at any desired speed, walking for recovery after each.	Indoors—repeat day 1 substituting 66-88 pound barbell for medicine ball and 36 inch hurdles for low hurdles.	Outdoors and Indoors—30-45 minutes easy running outdoors. Indoor pickup sprints, starts, hurdles, and medicine ball throwing of day 1.	Indoors—general body development with exercise desired: handball, easy pickup sprints, starting exercises, medicine ball throwing, weight training and easy jogging.	Outdoors—90 minute training in woods, repeating many 800-1000m runs. Starting exercises at maximum explosiveness.

January-February—Similar training to that described above with increased intensity. Speed of runs increased, barbell weight increased to 132 pounds and the number of medicine ball throws and pushups increased 20 times from a deep trunk bent forward position, throwing the medicine ball up to the ceiling, 10 pushups with the right and left hand.

March-April—4 outdoor and 2 indoor workouts weekly during March. Outdoor workouts entirely beginning April. Running intensity increased with training similar.	30-minute jogging and calisthenics, jumping using springing steps, 6-8 X 30m sprints walking for recovery, 6-8 X 120m at 12 seconds 100m pace, walking for recovery, 200, 300, 200, 300, and 200m repetitions of easy striding walking between. Warm-down jogging.	Warmup jogging—calisthenics, 12-15 X 30-35m sprint starts without gun, 6 X 150m at 12.5 100m speed with recovery walking. Medicine ball throwing, light weight lifting, hurdling on the grass.	Easy running jumping and throwing according to desire, 4 X 200m in 25-26 seconds with 200m walk after each. Jogging for long period of time.	Warmup jogging — calisthenics, 3-4 X 120m pickup sprints, walking 120m after each, 5-6 X 40m sprints walking for recovery, 10-15 X 25-30m sprint starts. Medicine ball, jumping, and use of light weights and shot, 4-5 X 150m pickup sprints at 7/8 speed, jogging.	Repeat day 3.	Running in a park or woods on grass. Warmup jogging-calisthenics. Running start 50, 60, 100m runs, 30-35m sprint starts, 2 X 150m in 11.5 100m pace, 2 X 200m at 24.0 seconds walking for recovery. Warm-down jogging.
May-June—devoted to form building. With a weekend race only 3 workouts are used terminating training on Wednesday.	Warmup jogging—calisthenics, 4-5 X 40-50m sprints walking between, 2-3 X 120-150m pickup sprints, 6-8 X 40m sprint starts, 3 easy and 3 fast, 3 X 50m from running start in 5.0 to 4.8 (and later 4.8 to 4.6) walking after each.	Warmup jogging—calisthenics, medicine ball throwing, jumping. Running according to desire which may include easy pickup sprints, easy starts, and warm-down jogging.	Usual warmup, 3 X 120-160m pickup sprints walking between, 2 X 50m sprints from blocks 3 X 50m from running start, 2 X 100m from runnining start, 1-3 X 200 m in 23.0 seconds walking for recovery after each.	Warmup, 3 X 150m pickup sprints, 3 X 20-40m maximum sprints, 2 X 50m from the blocks, 2 X 100m relaxed over first 50 and full effort over final 50m; 50, 60, and 100m sprints with easy running start, walking for recovery after each.	Rest.	Competition.

July—preservation of form.

Training for the 100-Meter Dash

Pre-race Warmup: 880-yard jog, 10 minute calisthenics, 3 X 150 at ½, ¾, and ⁹⁄₁₀ speed, walking after each repetition, 3 X 15 from blocks.

Season	Monday	Tuesday	Wednesday	Thursday	Friday	Saturday
November—Each workout preceded by warmup: 1½ mile jog, 15 minute calisthenics, 3-4 X 150 beginning at ½ speed and increasing.	20 X 220 in 28-31 seconds, walking 220 after each.	10 X 440 in 72 seconds, jogging 440 in 3½ minutes after first 5, walking 440 after each of last 5.	5 X 660 in 1:42-1:45, walking 660 after each of first 3, 880 after fourth.	25 X 220 in 28-31 seconds walking 220 yards after each.	Same as Tuesday.	Rest.
Winter—On wood track 12 laps per mile. Warmup: 880-yard jog, 10 minute calisthenics, 6 X 75 at ¾ speed, jogging 70 yards after each.	4 X 293 in 35 seconds, walking 3-5 minutes after each; 6 X 75 at ⁹⁄₁₀ speed from running start jogging and walking after each, 6-10 starts for 10 yards, decelerating for 30 yards.	660 in 1:32, walk 5-11 minutes, 2 X 293 in 35 seconds, 6 X 75 at ⁹⁄₁₀ speed from running start, jog-walk 70 yards after each; jog 440, 6 starts as in Monday's workout.	15 X 75 at ⁹⁄₁₀ speed from running start, jog-walk 70 yards after each.	6 X 75 from running start at ¾ speed with 70 yard walk-jog after each.	Rest.	Competitive race.
Summer—Warmup; 1½ mile jog, 15 minute calisthenics, 3-4 X 150 starting at ½ speed and increasing after each repetition.	660 in 1:25, walk 5-10 minutes, 10 X 150 at near full speed from running start walking 150 yards after each, 300 in 32.5.	4 X 300 in 31-32.5 walking 10-15 minutes after each.	6 X 150 from blocks walking 3-5 minutes after each, 20 X 35 yard sprint starts.	6 X 150 at ¾ speed from running start, walking 150 yards after each.	Rest.	Competitive race.

F.
PERSONAL RECORD
SHEETS

Test Scores and Training Programs

Name_____ Height_____ Weight_____

Starting Date_____ Major Attack Points:

____ Starting ability   ____ Stride Rate

____ Acceleration   ____ Anaerobic Fitness

____ Stride Length   ____ Strength/Power

Test Item	Date	Initial Test Score	Minimum Standard	Post-Test Score	Improvement
40-Yd. Dash (Stationary)					
40-Yd. Dash (Flying)					
50-Yd. Dash (Flying)					
100-Yd. Dash (Flying)					
300-Yd. Dash (Flying)					
440-Yd. Dash (Flying)					
Anaerobic Capacity					
Stride Length					
Stride Rate					
Arm Strength					
Leg Strength					
Flexibility					
Body Fat					

Strength/Power Record Sheet

Exercises	Sets	Record of Each Workout								
		Repe-titions	Weight	Repe-titions	Weight	Repe-titions	Weight	Repe-titions	Weight

Workout Schedule

Week	Days	Exercise Program	Duration		Workout Description	Weight
			Time	Distance		

G.
THE COMPARATIVE
SPEED OF ANIMALS
AND HUMANS

Normal and Maximum Heart Rates and Running Speed of Animals

Animal species	Normal heart rate (beats/minute)	Maximal heart rate (beats/minute)	Running speed in mph
Ass	40	56	30
Beaver	140	—	approx. 40
Camel	25	32	9.7
Cat	120	140	30
Cattle (bos cavus)	35-40	45-50	—
Cattle (dairy)	60	70	—
Cheetah	55	65	70
Chipmunk	684	660-702	approx. 40-50
Dog (canis familiaris)	70	120	—
Dog (greyhound)	80	90	40
Dog (St. Bernard)	74	80	approx. 25-30
Elephant	41	50	25
Fox (gray)	122	150	40
Fox (red)	122	150	approx. 35-45
Giraffe	66	—	approx. 50-60
Horse (nag)	37	32-44	15
Horse (thoroughbred)	38	45	45
Lion	40	—	43-50
Man	72	2½-3 times normal	approx. 25.6
Mule	46	50	approx. 10-20
Panther	60	—	60
Rabbit (lepus)	251	167-330 anesthetized	approx. 45
Rabbit (l. cuniculus)	120	160	approx. 45
Skunk (striped)	166	144-192	approx. 40
Squirrel (ground)	140	400	approx. 40-50
Tiger	64	—	50-60

SPEED AND EXPLOSION VIDEO CASSETTE

Revolutionary techniques for increasing your speed in short distances for team sports visually demonstrated on a 49:22 min. video cassette. Designed for football, basketball, soccer, baseball and track, the program is currently being used by the Dallas Cowboys and other NFL teams, U.S. Olympic Training Center, Professional baseball, basketball and soccer teams and universities, and high schools throughout the U.S. .

FEATURES: ☐ Tom Landry ☐ Bob Hayes ☐ Tony Dorsett ☐ Randy White ☐ Doug Donley ☐ Bob Breunig ☐ Bill Bates ☐ Brian Baldinger and other Dallas Cowboy Players.

EFFECTIVENESS: By following the methods presented athletes have produced more than 5/10 sec. improvements in 40-yd. dash times.

PREPARED BY: Dr. Bob Ward, Physical Conditioning Coach, Dallas Cowboys and Dr. George Dintiman, International Authority of Speed Improvement for Team Sports.

TO ORDER: Complete and return the form below with your check or money order.

Please send ____ 'SPEED AND EXPLOSION" Video Tape(s) @ 89.95. I am including $5.00 additional for postage and handling.

☐ VHS ($89.95)   ☐ BETA ($89.95)   ☐ 3/4 ($129.95)
☐ PAYMENT ENCLOSED: ____Check ____Money Order
☐ Charge to my: _____Visa   Master Care _____
   Credit card number _____ Expiration date _____
   Signature _____
PLEASE BILL ☐ (Institutions Only) Purchase Order # _____

SHIP TO: **Bill TO:** (if different)
Name _____   Name _____
Address _____   Address _____
City _____   City _____
State _____ Zip _____   State _____ Zip _____

MAIL THIS FORM TO:

LEISURE PRESS

LEISURE PRESS
P.O. BOX 3
WEST POINT, N.Y. 10996